PARENTS & COACHES

" Unleash Your Children's Inner Entrepreneur"

PARENTS & COACHES

"Unleash Your Children's Inner Entrepreneur"

To God for giving us the opportunity to be the voice of children and to our inspiration: our extraordinary parents who have dedicated their lives to making us successful and happy.
We love you, thank you!

To God for giving us the opportunity to be the voice of children and to our inspiration: our extraordinary parents who have dedicated their lives to making us succesful and happy.

We love you, thank you!

Original Tittle:	**Layout:**
Parents & Coaches	Steven Charris
1st edition	Todo Artes Publicidad
Publisher:	**ISBN**
Dreams Publisher	978-0-692-64444-7
Authors:	**Cover Design:**
Karen Carvajalino M.	Carlos Velez
Daniela Carvajalino M.	
Stephanie Carvajalino M.	**Cover photography:**
	Imran Nasser
Barranquilla - Colombia	

No part of this publication may be reproduced or transmitted in any form or by any means, mechanical or electronic, including photocopying and recording, or by any information storage and retrieval system, without permission in writing from the author or publisher (except by a reviewer, who may quote brief passages and/or short brief video clips in review.)

info@parentsandcoaches.com
www.parentsandcoaches.com

Index

Preface 7

Authors' Note 9

Chapter 1: 15
And the story begins

Chapter 2: 31
Love with conditions, entrepreneurship without passion

Chapter 3: 45
Is my child an entrepreneur?

Chapter 4: 61
Why raise entrepreneur children?

Chapter 5: 77
Today we need more than just parents

Chapter 6: 95
Neurolinguistic Programming: An essential tool

Chapter 7: 113
Beliefs

Chapter 8: 125
The Triune Brain

Chapter 9: 135
The Family

Chapter 10: 145
The influence of media, friend and school on a young entrepreneur

Chapter 11: 157
Financial education

Chapter 12: 169
What time is it?

How to Identify your Type of Brain (Tests) 180

References 188

About the Authors 191

Connect With the Carvajalino Sisters 193

Preface

Once upon a time there were three little girls called Karen, Daniela, and Stephanie. They were six, seven and eight years old. This is not a fairy tale in fantasy kingdoms protecting vulnerable creatures. This is a story of three entrepreneurs who started when they were very young in the beautiful and historic city of Cartagena, Colombia.

The young entrepreneurs are now nineteen, twenty, and twenty-one years old and already own four companies. Their first book went around the world telling their story. With this book, they are publishing a true innovation in entrepreneurship and financial education. The sisters have become a phenomenon of success for youth and a role model for families and schools.

Great people always have great people behind them. In this case, Luis Manuel Carvajalino and Elvira Martinez are the parent-coaches of these three authors and business women.

What techniques did Luis Manuel and Elvira practice? A fusion between Neurolinguistic Programming from Bandler and Gringer and the Triune Brain by W. De. Grégori. Luis and Elvira focused on an education directed towards action, which is located in the central brain.

The Carvajalino family is an entrepreneurial family. They own a private school, Cartagena International School, where students are educated with Neurolinguistic Programming and Triune Brain techniques, prioritizing the central side of the brain to raise entrepreneurs. I am talking about an alliance between family and school and the art of assembling neurons to create entrepreneurial geniuses. All this resulted in the phenomenon of Karen, Daniela, and Stephanie. If you want to know more, visit www.cartagenainternationalschool.com

This amazing integration of family and school, with the unification of paradigms, didactics, and goals had to be franchised and globalized. This is the background of the revolutionary book you hold in your hands. The young authors decided to reach parents to teach them to be the coaches of their children.

Parents and Coaches (www.parentsandcoaches.com) is a book from the viewpoint of children presenting their parents with new tools and techniques, begging that they use them for financial education of entrepreneurs and good citizens.

This precious manual is much-needed and should touch every family in the world. Besides the motivating and practical content, this book is written with Chococar's flavor, the first chocolate company of the young ladies. These girls are the vanguard of this century. I wish success to the three sisters and to their wise parents for this renovated educational proposal and for their example of entrepreneurship for youth.

Dr. Waldermar De Gregori
Adapter of the Triune Brain Theory

AUTHOR'S NOTE

Do you feel that your child doesn't trust you enough? Are you worried that you don't give them the attention they deserve due to work? Would you like for your child to be more like you, but they aren't? Are you worried about your child's laziness and lack of interest in their studies? Have you ever scolded your child because of their studies, without considering that they may have other strengths? Do you think your child will follow your career footsteps? Have you ever considered that your child could be a successful entrepreneur? Would you like to learn about a system that allows you to answer these questions? We can help!

The times have changed, just like generations and countries. Technology has evolved in an impressive manner. Each day things are totally different from the previous one. Things have become more innovative and contemporary. One thing that hasn't changed is the traditional way in which parents educate their children. Parents are raising 21st century teens based on information and beliefs from the past century.

After analyzing all of these questions, most parents identify with at least one of these situations. If you are part of this percentage of parents, this book will undoubtedly teach you a process which will greatly benefit your children. The primary reason we decided to write this book is to share the benefits we received and the triumphs we shared as a family after deciding to start our financial life at an early age.

In this book you will find different experiences, stories, lessons, myths, paradigms, and teachings that we have had the opportunity to experience in our lives as young entrepreneurs. At the same time, you will discover the lessons that we have learned based on our mistakes, the problems we experienced, and the difficulties encountered in the process. We share all of these stories to identify the key role that parents and coaches have played (and still play) in our lives. They educated all three of us using the same philosophy, but in different ways. They took the time to identify the manner in which we each understand, comprehend, and learn in order to truly develop our talents and abilities. We want to show you how you can do the same thing.

Many of the experiences described in this book were lived at our pedagogical company Chococar. This is the kind of business that may be created by any child, any age, race or social status, and it is a business that does not need great amounts of money to start it. The most important capital in this business is a high level of energy and positive attitude, together with our parents' support. In our case, it was our parents who motivated us into creating our first business. They raised us in a way in which entrepreneurship was more than just owning a company. It was a lifestyle.

Furthermore, we want to demonstrate that it is possible to be a young entrepreneur, and that there are many successful teens who have made it extremely far with the guidance and support of their parents-coaches. You will find the stories of these entrepreneurial leaders, how their parents-coaches showed them the path to making their dreams into realities, and how these realities add social and economic value to our society.

We are in the 21st century, when it is not enough to be a traditional parent that cares for their child, pays for their studies, and feeds them. Today parents should be their children's coach. It is important for us children that our parents go beyond the normal requirements to coach us for the game of life. It is necessary for parents to become informed on how to talk to their children based on their way of learning. It is essential that parents today understand the difference between the true abilities of their children and the abilities that they want their children to have.

Chococar is the company we created when we were six, seven, and eight years old. A few months later, we became international speakers on topics such as motivation, leadership, entrepreneurship and productivity for young people, adults, parents, foundations, and public and private companies. After speaking with different audiences, we realized that the world needs to know about this new methodology in the education of children and young people. We are convinced that if parents like you make the decision to become Parent-Coaches to their children, we can contribute to the creation of a new society of young entrepreneurs for the world.

For this reason, on June 8, 2007, we decided to write our first book. This, ladies and gentlemen, could not have become a reality without the tenacity developed during our childhood, the strong desire to contribute our grain of sand to the world, and of course, to our Parent-Coaches who repeated to us every day that they believed in us. Their motivating words led us to continue writing and striving to bring forth a successful model for families, and especially to share the great benefits that we have had with talented children and young people with many skills to develop.

Childhood

Daniela

Stephanie

Karen

CHAPTER 1
AND THE STORY BEGINS...

It all started in February of 2002, when our parents told us the importance of developing our talents at an early age, and discussed starting our own business. Our parents told us it was important to start working on the foundation of our life project early to give us an advantage later in life. As girls aged six, seven, and eight years, we listened to our parents, but we did not give much importance to the issue. However, we did not entirely ignore it; the idea of creating a small family business lingered in our minds.

A few days later, we woke up early to go to school. After a long day of classes and extracurricular activities, we came home very tired with only one wish: to rest. Karen, the oldest of the three, went to sleep on the living room couch. Soon it was nine in the evening, the time when our parents had friends over. During the conversation, Karen woke up and heard the story that Claudia, a friend of our parents, was telling them. What she heard gave her great cause to worry. It was shocking for Karen to learn that after working for 20 years at the same company, Claudia had lost her job. The company for which she worked was downsizing and her contract was canceled. It was difficult for us to understand how they could lay off Claudia without considering the years of sacrifice, hard work and dedication she had given to this company. Claudia had dedicated most of her life to the same job. This allowed her to be an expert at her work, but at the same time had inhibited from learning to do other things. She was 45 years old, and it was difficult to compete in the labor market, due to the fact that many companies prefer young talent to occupy vacant positions.

From one moment to the next, Claudia became an unemployed person desperately seeking a quick manner to supply the fixed income she was accustomed to. Many questions went through our minds. What will Claudia devote herself to doing? How will she support her family? What is the point of working so much, if an offhand decision of another person may end with you unemployed? Where will she obtain the money to pay for her children's school? Claudia was not only affected by the lack of economic means, but she had also lost confidence and her self-esteem was below ground floor. In just one day her life had taken a big turn. She went from getting a paycheck every month to feeling insecure and obsolete in the labor market. This situation definitely sparked our interest in knowing all the advantages and disadvantages of being an employee and an entrepreneur. At the end of the day we were so young, but we knew that when we grew up, we did not want to go through Claudia's situation. We wanted to have the freedom and power to control our own destiny. We did not know how we were going to do it, but were sure that we would soon discover it.

Gradually we began to pay more attention to the world of entrepreneurship. Ever since we were small, we were always adventurous and independent. We loved being the best in everything we did and always stood out. As long as I can remember, our parents were entrepreneurs and always took us to work with them. We were involved, in some way or another, in the decisions and processes of their companies. Our favorite game was making lemonade and bracelets to sell to our relatives and neighbors. At home, we always saw our parents as leaders, which inspired us to follow that same path. At school, we loved being the captains of our soccer teams, the leaders of our study groups in class and any other activities we were involved in.

A visit to Catty's house
Not too long after the episode with Claudia we visited our family friend Catty's house. As we played, it was impossible to ignore a delicious smell coming from the kitchen. We discovered that Catty's older sister, Vanessa, was making chocolates. The curious thing about the situation is that when we asked her to

let us taste it, she said she could not because the chocolates were for selling. That chocolate mixture looked so delicious we asked Vanessa to allow us to help so that we could eat the chocolate left in the pot. She agreed, and so we helped to finish the mixture, decorate and pack the chocolates. An hour later she went out to sell them. When she returned Daniela asked her why she sold chocolates. She told us she did not like asking her parents for money, and that she used the money she earned to buy clothes and go out with friends.

When we arrived home, we told our parents what had happened in the afternoon playing with Catty, and what was more exciting; we told them that we learned how to make chocolates from Vanessa. In mid-conversation, Stephanie, the youngest of the three, told Dad she felt bad for asking for so many toys and now thought that if she really wanted them, she should earn money to buy them just like Vanessa did. Dad told her there was no reason for her to feel bad, and made us realize that without us noticing, they always made us do something to earn the toys they gave us, such as good grades, playing sports, winning a competition, or fixing our room. It was then that we realized all the contests our parents invented daily actually had a reason for being. Home contests like dance, speech, math, spelling, and cooking really had a reason behind them. Today we understand that our parents did not simply give us things, but that we did "work" for them, or rather earn them.

Between talks and discussions, we realized that there were many productive ways that we could use our free time. Our parents encouraged us to seek the best way to do something we liked which could give us something in return. Their mission was to motivate us to find something that would make our hearts beat, something to make us truly happy. For several months we signed up for drama classes, dancing, singing and even in different sports. Our parents also assigned responsibilities to us and made us carry out the process from something as simple as checking that the house was kept in complete order to the remodeling of a room. Today we understand that they had us do all these tasks in order to unconsciously develop new skills in leadership, responsibility, self-confidence, self-esteem, and especially to enable us to discover what fascinated us.

On the other hand, we also played Monopoly and Cash Flow; with these games we started learning the fundamental pillars of our current knowledge in business by playing. We learned about negotiations, strategy, properties, money management, and sales. We learned that the richest is not always the one who has more money, but the one who has more assets, which in the case of Monopoly were properties. We also learned that when one has limited resources, i.e. the money we started the game with, one should think very carefully about where to invest. With each game we realized the importance of having a steady income, which in the game is achieved through receiving a rent, because if we run out of money (cash) we are forced to mortgage our properties. Games like Monopoly taught us many lessons, which later became part of our daily lives. The brain learns by repetition and playing these games constantly helped us change our way of seeing money and opportunities while having fun.

As time went by, we began to relate everything with entrepreneurship: television, the conversations we had, classes at school, soccer games, and of course the constant motivation of our parents. After searching, we discovered that we really enjoyed the topic of entrepreneurship. Yes, while many girls our age dreamed of being doctors or models, we dreamed of being great entrepreneurs. That day we were filled with courage and together we decided to start our own business. But where should we start? Of course, we asked our parents who were the main reason for this decision. They said, "You will achieve any goal that you want in life if you work consistently to succeed." The truth is that we have never forgotten those words. Over the years they became part of our philosophy of life.

Once the decision was made, we asked our parents for help. They told us the first thing you need to start a business is a product or service. Together, the three of us brainstormed about the problems or needs in our community and came up with possible solutions or ways to meet those needs. After talking for a couple of hours, we realized the opportunity was in front of our eyes...chocolates! We loved chocolates and many other people did too. They were fun and easy to make. Thus, our first company engaged in the production and manufacture of chocolates was born.

We already had the product-now we needed the name. We thought of acronyms, combinations of our names, names in another language, names that meant something and others that meant nothing, but none included all the aspects we wanted our company to have. Finally we realized we needed a name that included the product we sold and referred to who we were. After thinking of many names, we looked back to the first name that we had thought of, "Chocolates Carvajalino." This name was very long and a little difficult to remember, so after so many attempts to join these two words we came up with...**Chococar!**

Having defined our product and our company name, we thought we were ready to start producing and selling. However, our parents told us we could not begin without first obtaining as much information as possible about the industry we were getting into, as well as all the details of our future business. To investigate, we went to Vanessa's home and asked her everything about making chocolates, starting from where to buy the raw materials to how to sell the chocolates. She took the time to teach us step by step how to make chocolates and gave us all the information we needed to make our business work.

After speaking with Vanessa we took out our first loan at the only bank that would loan money to girls aged six, seven and eight: "Dad and Mom Bank." They loaned us $30,000 Colombian pesos (about $10 USD) with which we bought 1 cooking pot, 1 kilo of milk chocolate, 1 kilo of white chocolate, 10 meters of ribbon, 3 dozen sticks and 100 bags to pack the chocolates. With all these materials on hand we were apparently ready to start earning money with our company; the truth is that we lacked organization. We did not know who was going to sell, who would buy the materials, who would keep accounts, etc. Our father explained the importance of dividing job positions and assigning responsibilities in a company. After our first board meeting (which our parents participated in) we decided to divide our positions based on strengths, weaknesses and types of brain. Karen, central brain, was chosen as General Manager. Daniela, left brain, was chosen as Commercial Manager, and Stephanie, right brain, as Sales Executive. We know this whole issue of the brain can be a bit confusing. It was for us at first, but in a few chapters we will explain what our father meant when he suggested we consider our brain type when choosing the job positions.

After dividing all the jobs, everything began to flow much better as each sister focused on what she liked to do and each one was responsible for a specific area. As general manager, Karen was responsible for the entire buying process, including finding suppliers that offered the best quality and prices. Trying to figure out the best place to buy was not an easy task, especially for an eight-year-old. Our parents' support was essential to make our dream a reality. They took the time to accompany us to different companies that Karen had previously called. In addition, they explained how to negotiate confidently with suppliers.

Our commercial manager, Daniela, was in charge of the advertising and finances of the business. After several drawings, Daniela finished the first draft of the publicity leaflet of Chococar, and she learned how to use Excel in order to keep track of sales, expenses, and profits. When we started thinking about where to sell our chocolates, the picture began to get complicated. Everywhere we went demanded documents and forms that we did not have. At first this discouraged us somewhat, but it caused us to realize we had our best market in front of us: our neighbors!

Before we started selling at our building, our parents told us to do a market research to determine what kind of chocolate would sell well. We understood this as going door to door and making a survey to see what was the favorite chocolate of our future customers. In the beginning, we decided to start our survey with neighbors whom we already knew, our parents, and some relatives. Afterwards we knocked on doors and offered free trials of several products in exchange for people's opinion. This strategy not only served as market research, but it was also a way to raise awareness of our company.

The general conclusion of our first survey was exciting. Most of our participants loved the product and gave us great advice for its improvement. One of our neighbors taught us that people tended to buy larger and thinner than smaller, thicker, chocolates. After this experience, we were convinced that chocolate was the perfect product for three very important reasons: 1. There was a great demand for our product. 2. Chocolates were easy to make and sell. 3. Our product had ample profits.

On the other hand, Stephanie began to practice new sales tactics because we wanted to expand into new market segments. Our parents spent hours and hours training us in what they considered an entrepreneur's success: selling. Selling is not an easy task, but our parents provided us with tons of motivation and confidence before each day's sales.

In this new era of entrepreneurship, we had to lose our

shyness, fill ourselves with confidence and go peddle to all our neighbors, door to door. At the beginning, it was somewhat uncomfortable. We didn't know how to make contact with people we did not know. We practiced how we were going to greet people and what jokes we would say a thousand times before knocking on a door. We had different strategies to connect with adults, young people, and children. The seconds between ringing the doorbell and someone answering the door were filled with millions of feelings. After repeating this same process many times, ringing, telling, and selling, this process began to become natural. Nervousness started to decrease and confidence to increase. Every door we knocked on became a different story. Some neighbors bought our product and recommended us, others told us to come back another day or that they did not care for chocolate at the time. All these experiences, especially being told, "No," helped us gain more confidence and find new ways to do whatever was necessary to get that person to buy.

Our neighbors were an excellent market due to the fact we didn't have to spend money on transportation or pay a commission to another company to sell our product. In our first week of operations we sold $200,000 Colombian pesos (about $70 US dollars.) At first we could not believe it! It seemed incredible that we, who were only six, seven, and eight years old, had produced two hundred thousand pesos in just five days. This provided a reason to continue selling and created a spirit of excellence and improvement in each of us.

When the time of reckoning came, Daniela subtracted the

expenses ($30,000 Colombian pesos) from the sales ($200,000 pesos.) It resulted in a net gain of $170,000 Colombian pesos (about $56 USD.) From that profit, she designated 40% to reinvest in the company, 10% for savings, 18% to pay the initial loan, and the remaining 32% for our personal account intended primarily to buy toys. After selling every week for a month, we went with our mom to open our first bank accounts. Depositing money we had produced by ourselves and having our own account cards was impressive and made us feel important. The truth is we felt like true entrepreneurs.

After several months we decided to expand our market. Now the school where we studied was our new target. We had a meeting with the school principal to tell her about the idea of selling our chocolates at the school cafeteria and she accepted. She asked us to bring a contract and that was all we needed to start. This was the first time someone told us to sign a contract; however, we knew we needed to show confidence and asked her to give us two days to bring the contract. Immediately after we left the office, we ran to call our parents to tell them about it and ask for help in drafting the contract. With this new market segment, our responsibilities increased as business opportunities expanded. Later we opened a new outlet at a private company in Cartagena, a city near where we lived.

Our company was gradually growing larger. It was important for us to grow with it, so our parents hired a lady to teach us new recipes for other types of chocolates. With all the negotiating skills that Mom and Dad taught us, we obtained a lower price for the raw material of our products. By expanding our line of products and lowering costs, our sales and earnings increased. At that time, we sold in outlets and had loyal customers who knew our products and placed orders for birthdays and other events.

After a year of work, Chococar had become a real company. Sales continued to increase and it was difficult for us to meet the demand for our products, comply with our academic responsibilities at school, and of course have time for fun simultaneously. This led us to make our first big decision in business: hire our first employee. This decision gave a total turn to our company, and we now had a greater responsibility, someone else depended on us. She was responsible for the production of chocolates while we were looking for more customers.

More than a business to gain money, **Chococar** became a learning platform for life. With **Chococar,** we learned valuable lessons about management, advertising, marketing, finance, and accounting in a business company as well as the values and principles that would direct our lives. We learned the importance of effective communication as we worked in a family environment where maintaining a good relationship between sisters/partners was vital. We learned terms and business processes that became the basis of our professional life. More importantly, we lived unforgettable experiences that have marked our history and personal life. Together, we strengthened values such as respect, solidarity, honesty, and of course sisterhood. We gained confidence in ourselves and developed the ability to dream bigger. We learned how to make decisions in times of crisis and understood the importance of smiling in the most difficult moments. Our self-esteem increased exponentially and we were sure that we had what it took to be successful. We had gained an intrinsic motivation that would not let us lose heart and urged us to give the best of ourselves. The lessons we learned each day from **Chococar** were definitely more valuable than money. Having had the opportunity to practice entrepreneurship in such a fun way from an early age gradually evolved into our lifestyle.

I DIDN'T KNOW YOU LIKED TRACK AND FIELD SO MUCH, I THINK WE MIGHT HAVE A FUTURE CHAMPION!
YES! THIS IS EXACTLY WHAT I WANTED, YOUR SUPPORT.

Our First Company: Chococar

CHAPTER 2
LOVE WITH CONDITIONS, ENTREPRENEURSHIP WITHOUT PASSION

They say our children and young people are the future of the world, but what are the parents of today teaching to ensure our children are better off than we were? How can we avoid the mistakes of the past and learn from them without experiencing them? What are parents doing differently from their parents so that we become better?

The lack of affection from parents to their children and the lack of communication between them tends to generate gaps in the lives of children and adolescents. The children who are affected by this situation are more likely to develop obsessions about situations, objects, or relationships with other people. When children affected by this situation receive a demonstration of affection, they often want to fill the void their parents unintentionally created in their hearts. Moreover, lack of trust in the family leads children to act recklessly. In many cases, children and young people tend to take anyone as confidant of their personal affairs regardless if these people really care about the child's welfare or just want to take advantage of a moment of weakness the child is going through.

Furthermore, the lack of support from parents creates mistrust in children that leads them to ask questions such as: If my parents are unable to believe in my dreams, why should someone else? Situations like these induce many children to create limiting stories that they gradually come to believe, and this is what unconsciously sets them apart from their goals and dreams. All of these are factors that negatively impact the life of a child and result in lack of confidence, low self-esteem and depression. These traits can reach worrying levels where children lose motivation and in some cases, even their interest in life. It is necessary for our society to understand that, to a large extent, a person's decision-making abilities and their lifestyle are based on the training and support they received from their parents when they were children.

Orphans with living parents

Some children do not feel their parents meet the role of living parents in their lives and feel orphaned. This has drawn our attention since we were very young, so we decided to probe further to the root of this problem. Our mother always told us that every situation in life has different perspectives and we need to look at all of them to better understand. For this reason we decided to analyze why most parents spend more time working than with their children. We began to read and ask the parents of our friends. In addition, we took our school's database and selected parents of children from different grades to ask their opinion on the subject. After a lengthy investigation, we came to the surprising conclusion that the primary reason why they spend so much time working is precisely because they want a better future and quality of life for their children. We asked young people and children what they thought about this situation. Again, we were surprised to see that the vast majority did not understand why their parents spent so much time working. On the contrary, many said their parents spent more time at work because they did not want to be with them or simply because this was normal and that someday they would do the same.

Many parents today sacrifice quality time with their children. They do not consider that one day when they want it back, it may be too late to recover a quality relationship with their children. Eventually the years pass and today's apple of your eye, or Mom and Dad's champion, for whom you work day and night to provide with a better future, will have grown and it will be their turn to form their own family. That is when a parent's time of playing the main character's role will be over. Parents can focus so much on building a future that they neglect the important issue, the present. It is this time when children live to share their lives with their parents. This is when children are ready for their parents to teach them how to form the basis of a future until they can take on that responsibility themselves.

Today, we invite you wholeheartedly to think whether it is

worth sacrificing millions of smiles and happy memories with your family. We're not saying you should quit working to spend more time with your children because we all know that bills are not paid with smiles. It is important to analyze this situation because it could sound unfair to parents whose ultimate goal certainly is their children's success. It is true that many children know this, but during moments of weakness when the child seeks support from his parents and cannot find it, this can lead to having thoughts that affect their self-esteem such as: Work will always be more important than me. Why do I strive to do things well if my parents are never going to be there to see? Maybe if I do something bad I will finally get their attention. I have to do something so that Dad realizes I exist, and that I need him.

We are in a new era where negotiation between parents and children is valid. Our parents always sat with us to talk about the projects they were working on. We learned basic business concepts from an early age from what they told us about their workday. They taught us how to negotiate and plan ahead for our important events and activities so they could be first in line to support us at our dance presentation or speech contest.

Talk to your children, embrace him/her, and flood them with love. Teens often act as if they do not need a hug. The truth is that every day they put up invisible signs that say in giant letters, "Dad, Mom, I need you. I do not want to say it, but I need you to hold me and tell me that everything will be fine." The most important opinion in the life of a child will always be their parents'. This is something that will never change. Parents, give yourselves a chance to think about those situations when you said you did not have time, when in a moment of rage, you sent your child away and told him/her to leave you alone. Think of those moments when you unconsciously thought it was a nuisance or were too tired to hear their stories. Today, from the bottom of our heart, we say: cherish your child...you are still on time.

Love with conditions, entrepreneurship without passion

We think the best way to explain how someone can feel orphaned with living parents is with a real example, so we decided to tell the story of our friend Sebastián. He is an eighteen-year-old young man who grew up in a family whose focus was their parents' work. Other activities that did not allow them to devote much time to their children. We do not believe that work is bad, but there must be a balance between work and family. For Sebastián, his parents thought that providing a home, food, and education for their children was enough, and that their work as good parents was accomplished. Over time, Sebastián got used to the fact that his parents did not demonstrate affection with hugs and kisses. It became a routine to see them a few seconds a day before they left for work and to exchange a few words when they arrived home at night tired and ready for sleep after a long day at work. He understood that this was his reality and decided to adopt a positive attitude to face it.

Sebastián has always been a young entrepreneur. We remember that he always wanted to sell everything that he could and asked for discounts before buying anything. One day, Sebastian realized that he had all these negotiating qualities and decided to start a business. He had many resources such as capital, time, and willingness. However, he lacked something very important: the unconditional support of his parents, one of the fundamental requirements for a young entrepreneur to be successful. In the process of creating and solidifying his company, Sebastián realized that his parents were not present when he needed them. His parents were always busy, had something better to do, or in his words, did not take him seriously. Sebastián realized that in many cases his parents made up excuses to avoid talking about his company. This made him think that they were not aware of the importance that this project had for him. The young man tried to obtain his parents' attention in many ways, and found that the only way to get their attention was showing them how they would benefit from doing so.

One day Sebastián asked his father to accompany him to a business meeting and his father answered that he could not go because he was exhausted from work. This discouraged Sebastián because he knew his father had more experience than he did, and that the presence of an adult provided much more credibility. Sebastián was surprised when he arrived home and saw that his father was not there. He had gone shopping with his sister. At this moment Sebastián wondered: Was my father really tired? Does spending time with me seem boring to him? Does my father love my sister more than me? Is what I am doing not important to him? Are my goals meaningless for him? Does one child deserve more love than the other?

That day Sebastián realized that his father's love was

conditional. Nevertheless, Sebastián does not hate his parents. He cannot, nor does he want to. He appreciates that they gave him the opportunity to live, gave him education, clothing, and food, but he understands they ignored him when he needed them most. Sebastián loves his parents and thanks God every day for them, yet it is clear he cannot find support from them to accomplish his dreams.

Sebastián was part of the large percentage of adolescents who have communication problems with their parents. He was one of those young people who seem perfectly fine in front of other people, but inside are really craving love. He usually liked to go to parties and was known as a humorous person who had no problems. If he had not told us his story, we would have never imagined that the real reason he liked to go to parties was because it was a place he could temporarily forget his problems.

One of those days in a young person's world where everything goes wrong and everyone is against you, Sebastián was very sad and discouraged because things in his company were not going well, he was losing money, and worse than that-things in his personal life were not good. He was tired of looking for support from his parents because he knew they would not pay attention to him. On that same day, he went to one of those parties where he went in search of the refuge he could not find at home. Unfortunately, he found himself tempted by his friends to commit criminal acts. As his friends were the only ones who payed attention to him, Sebastián thought they were his true support and the only people who truly cared about him. His "friends" convinced him that the best choice was to earn "easy money" instead of working and devoting so much effort into his business. His frustration, coupled with the emotional weakness, bad friends, and lack of parental support led him to make the wrong decisions, and he ended up in jail.

Today, Sebastián is another example of how parents can unconsciously destroy their children's dreams by offering them conditional love. It is very painful for a child to lose a great opportunity to share either great or small achievements with their parents. We understood that life is an ongoing process, and having been accompanied by our parents during childhood is the reason why we know many successful adolescents. On the other hand, constant parental absence is the reason why many young people do not dare to fight for their dreams, or do not even have dreams or anything they are passionate about. Education and parental support is a key factor in developing strong character and personality traits such as self-confidence. Parents play a key role in building a child's identity as well as the fears and prejudices with which they grow.

Siblings Vs. Siblings

> YOU HAVE TO BE LIKE YOUR BROTHER. HE ALWAYS GET GOOD GRADES

Many homes today have become "boxing rings" for many siblings. Besides the usual fights between siblings, parents unconsciously create situations that generate resentment and anger among their children. Here is a list of the most common situations:

• A child has more resemblance to one of the parents than the rest, and the parents unintentionally give some preference to that child. This arouses jealousy in the other children, which results in constant bickering and meaningless future resentments.

• The next case is more common in Latino families. When the

siblings are a male and a female, the male is allowed to do many more things simply because of his sex.

• When parents have several children and allow the eldest to impose his criteria over his siblings or when the youngest child manipulate his or her parents by crying to obtain whatever the eldest did not. Also, in case there are three siblings, when parents pamper the youngest child as the baby of the house, and/or give more freedom to the oldest because he has to learn how to be responsible, then the middle child is too big to be pampered and yet is too small to be given the freedoms that the eldest gets. Immediately, the middle child sees this as an injustice and may think it is because their parents prefer their siblings.

• One of the most common actions taken by parents is to make comparisons between siblings. For example, "Why aren't you like your brother, who does well in math?" These comments greatly damage relations between siblings, affect children's self-esteem, and generate insecurity. Comparisons negatively affect children's personality and character development. For the child who is praised, self-esteem goes beyond limits, and this can cause them to become arrogant and vain. These comparisons make siblings feel like enemies.

In many cases, parents inadvertently induce fights between siblings. Over the years they create closer relations with one child than the others, fueling resentment and converting their home into a boxing ring. In the same way that boxers are injured, many times children end up badly injured. This issue is worrying because it affects a large percentage of families today and in the future the impact may be more serious than imagined. We invite you to review the list and analyze how your situation is at home. Are you encouraging fights between your children without realizing it? Did this happen to you as a child and you are repeating the story? Are any of these situations affecting your relationship with one of your children? What are you willing to do to change this situation?

The Importance of Effective Family Communication

It is a nightmare to live in a house where everyone participates in activities independently and the few moments spent together as a family are full of fights and arguments. It is very difficult to live in a home where the day begins without saying good morning or where a meal is not shared at least once a week. Based on the research we have done and the compilation of stories of young people with whom we have spoken, we have realized that many young people are negatively affected by their parents, people who love them, but who become obstacles in achieving their goals.

Bad relationships at home significantly affect the lives of both parents and children in different ways. Many of us have friends who say that asking their parents anything is difficult. They often respond with things like: "Not right now, I'm on the phone, please do not interrupt me, I'm working now." On other occasions, they simply will not tell them anything because they are not at home. Our friends and classmates also told us how their parents sometimes answered when they finally got their attention: "What do you want? Now, what happened? Tell me quickly." This type of response immediately changes the course of the conversation and diminishes the desire to tell them things.

Sebastian told us that he remembers a day when he was seven, and was jumping on his parents' bed and in one of his jumps he fell and cut himself on a glass table that was next to the bed. His biggest concern was how he was going to tell his parents that he had broken the table. Who would he tell first? Who would not scold him? He was so concerned that he almost did not feel the pain of the injury. However, Sebastián's biggest surprise was when he decided to leave the room and his parents saw the wound. They ran to see what had happened to him. This was one of the few times when they did not scold him. The fear that Sebastián felt had been caused by previous situations when his parents had not taken the time to listen to his reasons, but immediately scolded him for things he had done.

Sebastián had always thought his parents were simply "complying with their duty as parents." Even if this was not true, the way that Sebastián was raised made him think so. The best way to overcome this situation is to generate discussions between parents and children to fix the problem as soon as possible. It is not fair that the great efforts made by parents to raise a family can be negatively affected because the right decision to solve these communication problems was not made on time.

It is very important to children that parents listen to their dreams and give support to achieve goals. Dear parents, let us repeat that the most important thing in a child's life is the opinion of his/her parents. Having a parent who understands you and believes in you and your abilities is invaluable. The joy children feel when they receive expressions of love and affection is indescribable. These tokens of affection turn into an engine to become a better person every day and have a strong desire to make their parents proud.

CHAPTER 3
IS MY CHILD AN ENTREPRENEUR?

From a very young age children begin to show their talents. It is extremely important to children that parents encourage the development of those talents because receiving parental support at such a young age is priceless. There is no magic pill or specific examination to help parents discover the talents of their children. This work consists of paying close attention to their interests every day, and recognizing what they like to do when they are not in school.

To identify our talents, our parents enrolled us in various extracurricular activities and we were constantly involved in different events. They listened to what we liked to do and allowed us to explore these areas. They never imposed anything upon us. We believe if they had obligated us to practice something we did not like things would not have worked, as the key to participation in all of these activities was that we wanted to do them and enjoyed each one of them. Since I was a kid, I practiced soccer, basketball, skating and swimming, but sports were definitely not my thing. However, these were fun experiences that I remember with great pleasure today. On the contrary, my sister Stephanie was very good at soccer and Karen at volleyball. As a child, I loved going to support my sisters at their tournaments to see how Stephanie was for my dad a sort of Messi or James Rodriguez of today. On the other hand, Karen has always been competitive and continuously brought home a neck full of medals. Consciously or unconsciously, our parents made each game an experience that was full of emotion and made sure it was a pleasant family time.

My parents understood that sports were not what fascinated me, so they never attempted to force me to like them. Instead, they supported what I liked: acting and performance. It is vital that parents understand siblings have their own personalities and talents. This avoids unnecessary competition between siblings and allows for a good relationship at home. The environment in which my sisters and I grew up was always stimulating and open. We had many options and we learned continuously. My parents aroused our curiosity and desire to explore, which motivated us to be the best in everything we did. As the years passed, my parents gave us the opportunity to try different areas, such as: ballet, crafts, textiles, cheerleading, and horseback riding. We even had our own percussion band!

Interests change, children grow and talents evolve
As time goes by, children become older and like different

things. One day they are interested in something; the next day they have no interest in that subject. On the other hand, many of those things start turning into passions, and those passions become competencies (skills or abilities.) Identifying those talents early allows them to evolve and advance. Most athletes discover their talents from an early age and begin practicing with the dream of becoming a professional athlete. Similarly, many people show their interest in entrepreneurship indirectly from an early age. Parents need to identify and develop this important competency. We have heard many cases of extraordinary children whose parents ignore their qualities or do not give enough importance to the great potential they have. It is crucial that parents do not underestimate a child's potential in the business world and understand that it is never too early nor is there an age limit for entrepreneurship.

Fine line between motivation and pressure

Motivation is the key in the process of optimizing our talents. Motivation is the engine that compels us to start and pushes us to finish an action. This can be internal to a person and is known as intrinsic motivation, or it can be from an external source and is known as extrinsic motivation. A large component of extrinsic motivation in the life of a child or young person are his/her parents. The parents' opinion means everything to children and young people. Even though we do not admit it all the time, the truth is that unconditional parental support is critical for our success.

Sometimes people make the mistake of turning motivation into pressure. Although the two words are very different, the actions are frequently confused. Understanding the difference between them can have a huge impact on whether or not a person receives the results they want. Motivation from parents consists in fomenting their children's talents in a positive way to lead them to act upon internal motivation and by their own choice. In contrast, pressure is a negative motivation that aims to foster a talent and leads the children to act in order to please their parents or comply with some commitment. In some cases, pressure just leads to frustration that turns into inaction.

When parents decide to help their children in the development of a talent or ability, especially entrepreneurship, it is very important that they reinforce the positive actions of their children in the specific areas they are working. It is demonstrated that positive reinforcement of an action encourages the repetition of a behavior. The key for our success was that our parents presented us with different opportunities to develop and discover new skills while we had fun. It is essential that children be supported in their passions, even if parents disagree. Catalina is a classmate that I had in fifth grade. One day, she told her parents that she wanted to be more adept at counting money because she always had a hard time calculating the change cashiers gave her. Her parents enrolled her at a mathematics academy because they saw the opportunity for her to improve that ability. This was the perfect tool for her to boost her academic performance. Catalina did not like math at all and every day she "hated" it more since she had to spend over 5 hours a week at a place where she only saw mathematics.

Catalina tried to convince her parents on many occasions to stop sending her to this academy, but they did not agree. She enjoyed soccer, so she tried to negotiate with them by telling them if they enrolled her in a soccer academy she would study hard to understand math and get better grades. Her efforts were unsuccessful. Over the months, Catalina's frustration and anger increased and her academic performance decreased. Catalina's passion was soccer. She was on the school team, and I can certainly say that she transformed herself when she was near the ball. She often told me that she was very sad because her parents did not support her dream. Her parents were determined that she would become better at what they wanted, and did not realize that their daughter had other talents. They believed that imposing mathematics was the best way for her to improve her grades and develop a skill that was "worth it." They said that soccer was a masculine sport and it was not good for anything, so they never went to watch her games.

Catalina was so discouraged, the coach called her parents and asked them to attend the tournament's final game. Catalina's parents attended the game and saw a side of their daughter they did not know. That day, after seeing the great talent and passion she had for the sport, their opinion about Catalina and soccer changed radically. From that moment on, her parents realized the mistake they were making and decided to support their daughter completely to reach her soccer-related goals. At the end of the year, her parents were surprised that she was awarded the best student in the class. She also received a scholarship for excellent athletic performance. Today, Catalina practices soccer professionally in Spain, and is fulfilling her dream.

Our Talent

Shortly after founding our first company, Chococar, my sisters and I discovered that we had a very special talent: doing business! Without realizing it, Chococar had become our favorite game and favorite pastime. Our parents, who were the first motivators of this idea, soon realized that we loved to spend time and effort in our company and they gave us their full support. Mom and Dad are entrepreneurs, so they used every situation at their company to teach us, from the smallest things like what made a good employee, or how they were improving their customer service program, to how to perform the most important negotiations. They asked for our opinions. We were involved in making important decisions. On the other hand, our parents guided us in the process of getting information on how to produce, sell, and improve our product, but they never did things for us. Instead, they gave us the opportunity to explore, propose, make mistakes, and do things our way.

Is My Child An Entrepreneur?

My father always taught me that an entrepreneur is a creative and innovative person who has the ability to research and develop an idea, then put it into action in a profitable, consistent, and sustainable manner over time. There are two types of entrepreneurs. The first type we will call business entrepreneurs. They are those who identify an opportunity in the market and create a business from this idea. There are also talent entrepreneurs who develop their skills in a productive manner such as artists or athletes among others.

Many children show empathy for entrepreneurship from a small age. We will tell you some of the signs to recognize entrepreneurial attitudes in your child. The following are the characteristics that a child/young entrepreneur has and a few simple strategies to promote and stimulate the development of these traits in your child. These characteristics become patterns that set the stage for his behavior in the future. If a child adapts these behaviors from childhood, it is very likely that these will continue being present into adulthood.

Characteristics of a young entrepreneur:

1. Self-motivation, confidence, and independence
A young entrepreneur acts based on a largely intrinsic motivation. This feature usually occurs in children who do not have authoritarian, overprotective, or permissive parents. These children have high self-esteem and believe they can achieve whatever they set their minds to. They rely on their skills and make their own decisions. Examples are children who choose their own clothes or toys. They focus on an activity, they do not stop until they complete it and they do not need extrinsic motivation from a parent or teacher telling him to finish their projects. This feature leads to persistence, desire to overcome obstacles, and independence.

A person who owes much of his success to his self-motivation, confidence and independence is Blake Ross, founder of Mozilla Firefox. He created his first website when he was ten years old. Blake became interested in programming during middle school, and did his first internship with Netscape at age fifteen. During this internship, he lost interest in the browser that he was working on because the direction being given by the company America Online was not what he expected. Ross and his partner Hyatt envisioned a smaller, easy-to-use browser that would be popular, and at nineteen years of age Ross and his partner launched a successful web browser that is downloaded and used by millions of people every day.

2. Leadership

This characteristic is evident in children from the manner in which they socialize to the role they play in the classroom or with their friends. These children love to listen, give their opinion, and contribute ideas. They also strive to do things well and most of their friends see them as role models. They organize study groups in class or become leaders of their sports team and do an excellent job working with others because of their empathy. They also like to help their peers, have a great power of persuasion, and constantly solve problems they encounter.

Matt Wullenweg is a clear example of leadership. At eighteen years old, he led a project that ended in what is now known as WordPress, a content management system for creating webpages or free online blogs. Matt started with fewer than 20 users. After seven years and the help of other developers, he now has more than 350 million users and has become a celebrity in the world of computers.

3. Creativity and innovation

Entrepreneur children see the world differently. For them, imagination is unlimited, and creating things with their hands is part of their routine. Usually they use their imagination to solve problems or create new things to supply a necessity they currently have. Many children express their creativity by drawing or writing songs. Some have genuine ideas about the dinner menu or an innovative way to complete their school project. They do not enjoy being like others. In contrast, they want to make a difference.

Sara Blakely opened her first business just out of high school, babysitting for eight dollars an hour. Her next job was at Disney World. Soon after, she became a fax machine saleswoman. Sara discovered a problem that women experienced when they wore dresses or skirts and did not know what to wear underneath. Girdles were too noticeable, as well as underwear, and thongs were very uncomfortable. At the time, the options were limited-so she decided to provide a creative solution. Daring to think differently, she created Spanx, an intimate apparel and undergarment company for woman and men. Sara invested her savings of $5000 and she is one of the youngest self-made billionaires in the world.

4. Initiative, perseverance, and action

Children who have this characteristic have the spirit to start new things in everyday life. If their toy is broken, they try to fix it. They do many things without being asked by their parents. They are supremely focused on their projects and do not rest until they are finished. They have no fear of failure and get up if they fall. They are always driven by the presence of possible dreams or goals to accomplish. They are active at home and at school, participating in multiple activities.

A person who personifies initiative, perseverance, and action is the renowned actor and comedian Jim Carrey. At age ten, Carrey took the initiative and sent his CV (curriculum vitae) to The Carol Burnett Show. When Carrey was twelve, his father lost his job and his family went through extremely difficult times. A few years later he left school and went to work at a tire company. At fifteen, he presented his comedy for the first time. After hundreds of performances, his talent was discovered and today he is one of the most famous comedians in the world.

5. Identify and take advantage of opportunities

These are children who are constantly on the lookout for new things and are attentive to the situation around them. They are often restless and likely benefit from every situation. They find ways to gain advantages over their peers in school projects or sports activities, and try to negotiate with their parents. They look for an opportunity in every situation. Developing this characteristic from childhood gives these kids the advantage of naturally identifying opportunities in situations presented in their daily life. An excellent example of this is Kevin Plank, who was known in his youth as "the sweaty guy." These comments bothered him so much that he decided to transform the problem into a $3.2 billion business of what is known today as Under Armour.

6. Challenge oriented

An entrepreneur child has determination and character. He or she likes challenges and does not enjoy giving up. While his peers and classmates play video games, he is dedicated to completing a challenge. Once they achieve a goal, they discover a more ambitious one to engage in due to their constant desire for self-improvement. They are very competitive kids and they love to win. A challenge-oriented youth began looking for different options to supplement his salary at the age of seventeen. Fred DeLuca then started the restaurant with more branches than any other fast food chain in the world today, known as Subway.

7. Research: finding information and guidance
This characteristic can be identified in children who love to ask questions: What is this? Where did it come from? Who did it? When? How? As my mom would say these are the children who like to know everything and are even interested in adult topics, business companies, current news or the economy. When they do not have enough information, they seek guidance from their parents, teachers, or other available resources. Curiosity, exploration and discovery are part of their lives. Martin Sorrell is the founder of the renowned advertising company WPP. Sorrell showed an early interest for business. He used to read the Financial Times when he was 13 and going to school on the bus. He showed interest on his father's successful retail businesses and talked a lot about it with him. On Sundays he would get the sales manager's reports and even visit the shops with his father. Sorrow told his dad he wanted to go into business when he grew up and his father told him that he had to go to Harvard Business School. Sorrow listened to his father's advice and ended up attending to that school.

8. Generation of ideas and vision
This is a quality often seen in children who manage to see farther than their peers. These are children who have the

ability to see a solution where others merely see a problem, and they develop a plan to achieve their goals. Typically, this characteristic is observed in children who have innovative ideas, such as finding dual functionality in their toys. These children have the ability to generate business ideas, the capacity to visualize themselves in the future and to decide who they want to become. A young man who saw something where nobody could see anything was Mark Zuckerberg, who from age eleven started computer programming, and at age nineteen from his bedroom at Harvard University had the vision to make the world become more connected when he launched Facebook.

9. Taking risks and decisions

This characteristic is evident when the child makes decisions or even when he or she is playing because their "modus operandi" tends to involve calculated risks and tests their skills. You can identify these kids when they are playing board games and they sacrifice a move or something in the game in order to win. These kids are the ones who decide where the family is going to have dinner or which gift is better to buy for Mom or Dad's birthday. Risk is an indispensable factor in the business world and the fact of complementing that risk with a good decision is what makes the difference between successful and unsuccessful people.

A medical student had the goal to make technological advances accessible to society. At nineteen, he started his first company. He bought supply parts from leftover inventory from computer vendors and used them to improve the already existing computers in the market. With this idea and $1,000, Michael

Dell decided to risk everything. He gave up his college career and he revolutionized the world of computers from production to sales model. His business made six million in sales during the first year.

10. Sales oriented

A defining characteristic of an entrepreneur child is definitely their interest towards business, especially in sales. They have a greater understanding of money than other children their age. They are always looking for something to sell or an activity that will generate a profit.

Warren Buffet began delivering newspapers to make money at an early age and then used that money to buy Coca-Cola in six-packs for twenty-five cents, which he then resold for ten cents per bottle. At age eleven, he began working at his father's brokerage company, where he bought his first stock. Today he is one of the most successful investors of all times and the third richest man on the planet.

How I Can Develop The Characteristics of an Entrepreneur in My Child?

After reading these characteristics, do you identify any of them in your child? Many children have these traits naturally, but others do not. The good news is that absolutely all of these characteristics can be developed with time and practice, and parents play a decisive role in this process.

Ways to Develop and Promote These Skills in Your Child.

- Set clear and high but realizable expectations
- Show a positive attitude towards failure
- Include issues and challenges in the daily routine
- Teach simple business issues on a day to day basis, such as identifying good and bad customer service at a restaurant
- Be a good example and role model
- Spend time in sports or activities that require risk
- Help to set goals and follow-up on those goals
- Constant motivation
- Help your children find their own answers
- Encourage creativity
- Invite them to participate in decisions at home and ask for their opinion
- Encourage exploration and research
- Teach them to earn the things they want
- Teach them to think long-term and visualize themselves in the future
- Allow them to help with small projects and assign responsibilities
- Teach them to manage time effectively
- Reward them for goals achieved
- Teach basic concepts of negotiation and obtaining discounts
- Teach how to save and encourage them to spend half of their savings on toys or something they want while investing the other half in future businesses
- Do the exercise of taking your child to buy something at a low price and sell it at a higher price
- Stimulate problem solving creatively

- Allow them to make their own decisions
- Give them freedom to test their limits and master their fears
- Involve your child in your business if you are an entrepreneur
- Create an adequate environment for discovery and exploration

...SO, THESE ORANGES ARE PRETTY CHEAP, I COULD BUY SOME WITH MY SAVINGS, MAKE JUICE AND SELL IT TO THE PEOPLE THAT ARE ALWAYS TRAINING IN THE PARK. THEY LOVE NATURAL ORANGE JUICE, WHAT A GREAT IDEA!!

Talents

Karen-Cheerleading

Stephanie-Soccer

Daniela-Modeling

Carvajalino Sister's Musical Group

CHAPTER 4
WHY RAISE ENTREPRENEUR CHILDREN?

Children of the twenty-first century face a slightly different world than their parents faced. We wish to share with you a list of real situations that could be currently affecting your child or which could become a real obstacle for them in the not-too-distant future.

A Reality From Which Your Children Are Not Exempt

1. High percentage of young pregnant women
According to the World Health Organization, about sixteen million women, ages fifteen to nineteen, and roughly one million girls under fifteen give birth each year. That is nearly

eleven percent of all births worldwide. When we were younger, we thought this was merely something that happened in the world, but not to people close to us. In time, we realized that this is our reality, too.

2. The taboo of suicide

More than 800,000 people commit suicide annually. Every forty seconds someone dies by suicide in the world; however, the number of attempted suicides is much higher. Even more troubling, suicide is the second leading cause of death among young people between fifteen and twenty-nine worldwide. This means it is not a localized problem that only occurs in distant regions of the world. It is a global problem. Suicide is an issue that could affect anyone. The largest issue we face is that it has become a taboo subject. People prefer not to talk about suicide.

3. Alcoholism and drugs

Alcohol is a legal drug that can be found in every corner of the world. Other professedly illegal drugs were at one time harder to come by. Today they are attainable for all young people, even those who have never seen or thought of using them. The lack of interest from parents, hoping to escape family problems, low self-esteem in young people, and the desire to be accepted by a social group are the major factors that lead young people today to use these substances and eventually become addicted to them.

4. Lack of interest in studying and extracurricular activities

This is an issue that affects many of today's children, which parents and children alike downplay. Many teens go to school, come home, sleep, and wake up the next day to repeat the same routine without actively participating in activities. These are usually young people who wake up without a dream to work toward or a goal or achieve. They are not passionate about anything and nothing captures their attention. These young people have no interest in identifying what they like or want to do when they graduate from school. For this reason, they become part of the large percentage of young people who graduate high school and make the decision not to study anything in college because nothing catches their attention. That causes them to lose time and when they decide to recover it, others have taken their place and their opportunities in their desired career field. In many cases, they become just one more unemployed person or they get a job in a field they do not like simply to survive.

5. Study, get good grades, graduate, and get a good job

This statement goes beyond languages, countries and cultures. Parents and schools are raising their children with the mentality and the hope that once they graduate from college they will surely have an excellent job waiting, but reality is totally different. Well paying, good jobs with long holidays that parents dream of for their children are increasingly scarce, and there is greater competition each day. Young people are trapped in following this pattern of: study, get good grades and get that dream job. They neglect to develop activities that give added value. When they graduate, this chain is broken and they cannot find the desired job. They are not prepared to do anything other than what they studied for. They become one of many young people who possess a college education, but are forced to take any job they can find instead of working with their passions.

6. The retirement pension, an increasingly distant reality.

In most countries, the current retirement age is between sixty and sixty-five years old. This age has a tendency to increase with the passing of time. If this continues, your children will have to wait a long time to access their pension. They might not even be entitled to it. Many young people are unaware of this issue and do not work in the present to secure their future. Unfortunately, when they begin to desire retirement, they realize that there are still many years of working ahead of them.

Since we were small girls, our parents showed us enterprises as a system. It helped us understand that just like a coin has two sides, life has one side with all the situations that can prevent you from being successful are present, and another side full of opportunities for you to fulfill your dreams. By understanding the reality of the world we live in, we decide what actions to take.

The entrepreneurship project, a tool for success!

We are convinced that entrepreneurship is a solution to keep the minds of children and young people busy and away from negative influences that may harm them. The key to training this mindset is to begin during childhood due to the fact that from birth, children are like a sponge and absorb everything that they hear, see, and feel. Since our parents led us down the path of entrepreneurship from an early age, this allowed us to forge distinct personalities. Having had the cost versus benefit ratio made clear from an early age gave us the character to say no to things that may hurt us when making life decisions. The entrepreneurship project gradually became more a lifestyle than a financial path in life. It has kept us away from negative aspects of our society and has kept us concentrated on waking up every day, being happy, and motivated to achieve our goals.

Children or adolescents who know our entrepreneurship program are less likely to fall into illicit activities, which can generate all kinds of misfortunes and sorrows for themselves and their families. These children are overwhelmingly less inclined to turn towards drugs or crime because they are busy being productive and advancing their development. In the future, they will be busy discovering their strengths and weaknesses instead of picking up bad habits on the streets. If parents and children implement this entrepreneurship program together from an early age, they are far more likely to make successful decisions because entrepreneurs make decisions based on what is best for their personal development.

The key is to find something that motivates you to live each day

As you have read in previous chapters, we created our first company, Chococar, when we were six, seven, and eight years old. About a year after creating Chococar, we had the opportunity to meet a professor at a prestigious university in Colombia. We met him on our endeavor of selling chocolates door to door. The professor was quite impressed with children so young with the perseverance to sell chocolates door to door. He extended an invitation for us to address his class at the university, and share what we did with older students.

This first experience was extremely significant. It marked the beginning of our career as lecturers. This was the first time we spoke to a large audience of predominantly older people. Afterwards, we noticed that people were motivated by our story. Our example contributed towards many of these students feeling capable of starting their own business. We felt motivated, happy, and excited to know that our example could cause significant impact on the lives of others.

When we finished, they asked us about our experience on stage. We did not have enough words to describe all the feelings we had experienced in one day. Today we can describe it as a cocktail of nerves, motivation, expectation, improvement, and strangely, a little hunger. We discovered that talking about business was something that made our three hearts beat at the same rate. Helping people to believe in their dreams, like we believed in ours, had become our new mission in life. It was not easy to inspire immediate confidence in our audiences, but it was greatly satisfying to see the smiles on their faces at the end of a conference. The three of us realized that we loved public speaking and sharing our experiences. Thus, helped by our parent-coaches, we decided to start our career as speakers and carry the message of entrepreneurship to children, young people and adults around the world.

We began holding our conferences at schools because we thought we could direct ourselves effectively to children and young people of our own age. With the guidance of our parent-coaches, we began to shape our portfolio of conferences to include presentations on: family businesses, awakening the entrepreneur, starting a business without money, and the goal of sales.

Several universities in Colombia contacted us, requesting we give our conference on how to awaken the entrepreneur in all of us. This speech was a success. It was exciting and we were happy to see ourselves contributing to the life of university students. We have had the opportunity to be at more than nineteen universities in major cities of Colombia, Panama, Argentina and the United States.

We have participated in numerous international exhibitions, forums, and conferences. We like this type of scenario very much, with thousands of people giving us an opportunity to sell **Chococar** products. We discussed our venture project in Colombia with great personalities such as the ex-President of the Republic, the minister of education, and many mayors of the main Colombian cities.

We also had the opportunity to give many lectures at public and private companies in Colombia, concentrated in the areas of motivation and sales. Our parent-coaches helped us to gain connections at companies through their friendships and relationships. These were excellent settings to expose and improve our conferences. Each company added to our speaking experience and helped make us known in the business world.

After seven years in many different settings, and with the full support of our parent- coaches, we decided to make our business more official. We created our own training company, **Quality Line Training.** Today, our company continues to grow and consolidate in the market as an excellent alternative training for success. We manage a corporate portfolio and an educational one, with products such as training, outdoors training, speeches, and lectures, among others. **Quality Line Training** provides a revolutionary methodology that combines NLP techniques, triune brain, experiential learning, motivation and fun to transform the lives of the participants in our events. Our company is well-established and recognized for the outstanding results we achieve with our clients. We have been interviewed in many Colombian media as well as in major international media such as CNN, Univision, and Telemundo Internacional. We are in the planning stage of an online product; **Quality Line Training** continues to grow today!

Today we are nineteen, twenty, and twenty-one years old. We have been to many universities, colleges, and countries around the world. Each time, the audience is larger and increasingly diverse, and the only reason why we are sure that we dare to speak to any audience is the fact that we started this program early. Of course, getting to this point of security and confidence in our abilities to lecture was not easy. We needed many hours of practice, dedication, tears of frustration, repetition in front of the mirror, our parents, and among ourselves, but we improved our public speaking skills to the point of competence and mastery. It involved great sacrifices and long nights of reading, but we persevered due to our great motivation.

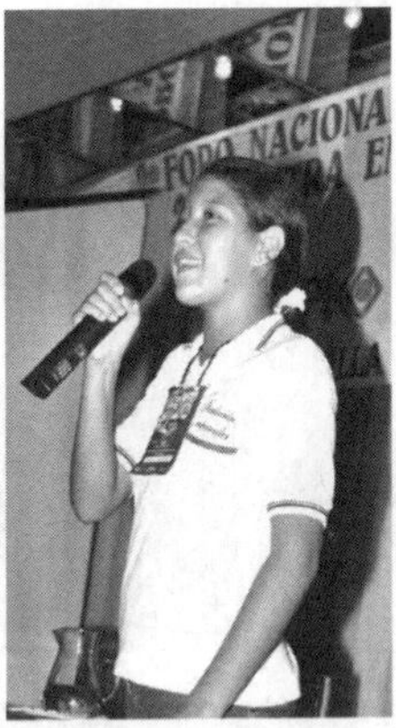

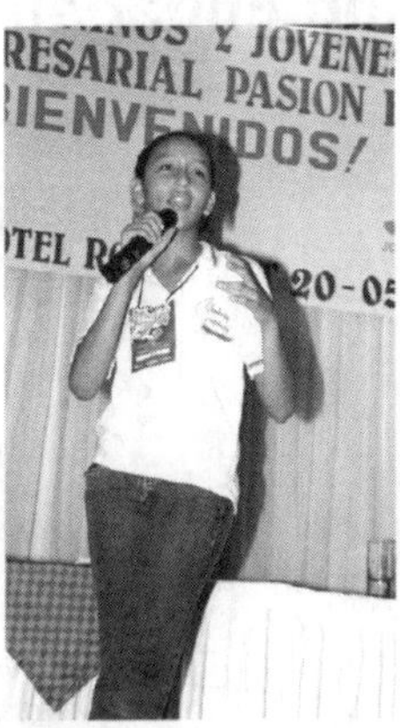
PASION

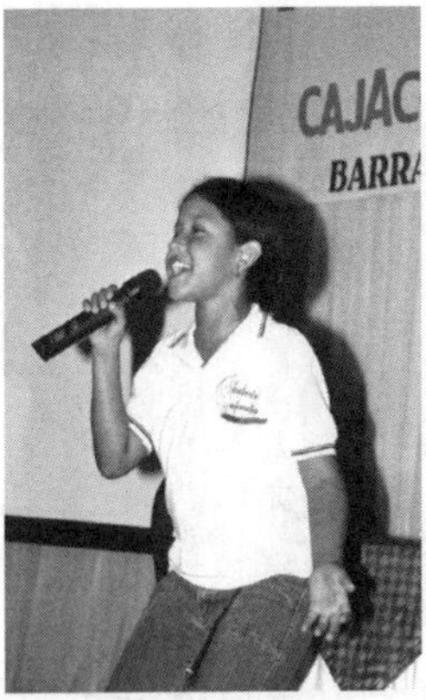

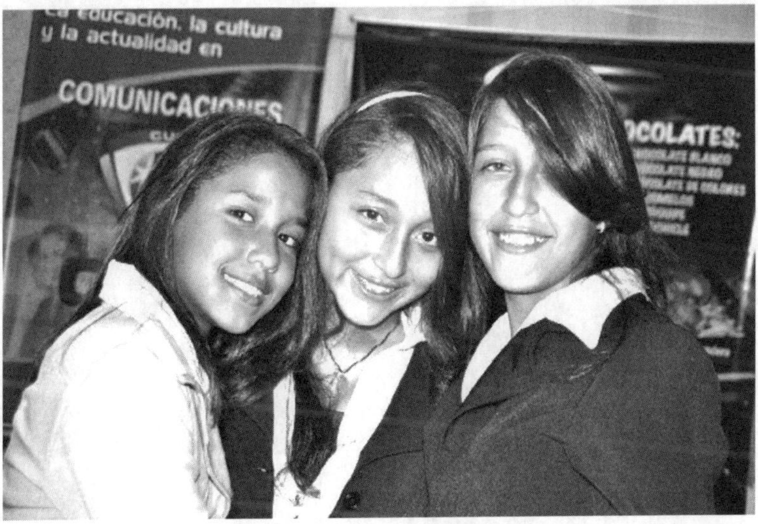
la cultura
y la actualidad en

Speaking Engagements

Beyond a business, entrepreneurship is a lifestyle

Coming home and doing nothing was never an option for us. If we did not have to practice for a conference we had homework and we had to spend time at our company. Selling chocolates door to door in our building became the way to lose shyness and gain confidence in ourselves. Losing embarrassment from speaking in front of others helped us in our work, personal, and school life. From that moment on, whenever a teacher asked who wanted to give a speech, offer acknowledgment, or lead an activity, our hands were always the first to go up.

Once you enter the world of entrepreneurship, you begin to see life from another point of view. You know the great feeling of getting up every morning in order to achieve a goal. To be motivated all the time and looking for new things to do distanced us from the vices that young people seek to vent their fears, sadness, or lack of skills. Entrepreneurship, rather than being a way to start Chococar or Quality Line, became a lifestyle. We developed the ability to look beyond the obvious, and we understood that we had to take advantage of the things happening around us. Due to the fact that our parents enrolled us in painting courses, swimming, dancing, and sports, we developed skills and learned the importance of always being engaged in something we enjoyed. We made use of whatever resources we had to find fun and productive activities.

One day our father brought home a home theater, the latest technology of the moment! The sound it produced was amazing and we felt like we were at the cinema. After enjoying many movies as a family, we decided to take advantage of the home theater. We went to all the apartments of the building with a list of three films and asked children what they wanted to see. After choosing the winner, we made a sign announcing the film, the date, and time it would be shown at our theater, called Cinecar. The admittance cost 1,000 pesos (about fifty cents at the time) and included a bag of popcorn. We left a few flyers at the lobby and others we slipped under the doors of our neighbors. The truth is that we did not expect many people; however, almost all the parents who lived at our building came to our home with their children. The first question we were asked was whether there was any responsible person in charge. Thanks to our parents who took on the responsibility for us, we had about twenty children at our first show.

With this story we want to show that entrepreneurship is something we live every day without realizing it. It accounts for many more benefits than just making money. If you analyze all the stories in our book, you will find lessons we learned from our experiences in each one. If we had not had an entrepreneurial mindset, we would never have taken advantage of all these opportunities.

Advantages That An Entrepreneur Acquires At An Early Age

We presented a list of negative situations that life presents every day to the young people of the twenty-first century. We invite you to understand that entrepreneurship is an immediate solution to remove children from these harmful situations. Here is a list of the most beneficial advantages we received from being young entrepreneurs:

1. We know our strengths and weaknesses and understand where we need to improve.
2. We have the ability to choose where to invest our time, what suits us, and what really does not appeal to us.
3. We are motivated by the idea of achieving our dreams. This motivation drives us to perform our personal, professional and academic obligations.
4. We are leaders; we distribute tasks to a group and demand results.
5. We have high self-esteem and trust that we can accomplish what we set our minds to achieve.
6. We have a strongly defined character and we know how to face situations positively.
7. We are young people with an understanding of culture; we want to have a general knowledge of current affairs.
8. We use financial mathematics and make negotiations that are favorable to us.
9. We have the ability to dream big, and have innovative and creative ideas.
10. We learn to work under pressure and make wise decisions in times of crisis.

There are so many more advantages. There are also some momentary disadvantages in life of a child or young entrepreneur. The biggest disadvantage with which we encountered was the fact that the banks could not give us loans or a credit card because we were underage. However, our parents signed as titleholders of our accounts and they taught us about the bank processes and how to lead an excellent credit life. We were aware that this was a variable experience. Through practice, we are now experts in the use of credit cards, loans, and investments. On the other hand, the lack of credibility on the part of other people had been a challenge for us. At the end of each sale or conference, we became more aware of how successful our venture was.

The biggest advantage is to start early!

During childhood, financial responsibilities are minimal if not nonexistent. Fears are less important than the desire to dream. Creativity has no limits and the negative beliefs and limitations created over the years do not have to be a major part of our daily life. Therefore, the risk of failure is much smaller and can be a source of learning. Time is on our side and providing the best possible way of using it is available to us. The famous disadvantage of the lack of experience can become our greatest asset. In thirty years, we will have a long history of experience and while others are just entering the business world, we will be considering retirement.

The most important thing for you to understand is that to achieve success as a child and young entrepreneur, parental support is essential. There is no doubt having had parents-coaches at our side all the time, to show us the best way, who gave lessons based on their experience to avoid making the same mistakes, motivated us every time we felt we could not go ahead. Their trust led us to understand that we needed to start working for our success at an early age.

POSITIVE ENVIRONMENT → YOUNG ENTREPRENEUR

CHAPTER 5
TODAY WE NEED MORE THAN JUST PARENTS

> Dear focus on studying and studying only, forget about being a singer. I wanted to be a singer as well and look at me, I am just a frustrated musician.

Many people proudly state that they are good parents who love their children and their children love them in the same way. While this is fine, in the twenty-first century it is inadequate to simply parent your children. The current circumstances require doing things differently with your family to face the challenges of this era.

In the past century, things did not change as quickly, nor did events move as fast. People had time to consider their options, to change their minds. Today's lightning-fast activities do not allow for such ruminations. One must make the correct decision as quickly as possible-and someone else might have made it first. Every day brings something new with it like new technologies, ideas, and innovations. For that reason, to be successful in today's world, one must be comfortable with the speed of change.

It is necessary for parents to understand that the way in which they raise, educate, and support their children will have an impact on their future. We lovingly, humbly say this and hope you can view the information we will provide in a positive light. Most parents want their children to have a clearly defined future from an early age; they want children who are winners and have the ability to succeed. The curious thing is that many want to achieve these goals using a traditional mentality: Study, be academically excellent, be the best in your class, study, study, study, graduate from school, and get a good job. This traditional mentality causes your child to develop different skills than those, which would be most useful and beneficial for him. Children who follow this mentality spend a lot of time studying to obtain a university degree in order to get a job. They do not consider that this plan is not guaranteed-consider the current situation in the world with respect to the high rates of unemployment and lower employment options available. This traditional path can lower your children's chances of success.

If you want your child to become a young entrepreneur with the ability to successfully shape their own development, you must play two roles for your children. Continue being the nurturing parent that succors and guides your children, and give them the encouragement and training they deserve in your role as a coach.

As parents, you are aware that you need to meet certain responsibilities: buying healthy food, providing clothes, taking them to places they need to go, providing a good education, teaching them many things about different subjects, looking after their health, teaching good manners, and spending quality time with them, among others. The role of a parent-coach is somewhat different from that of a conventional parent. What definitely does not change is the love with which a parent educates his children.

We understand that being a parent is one of the most difficult tasks ever and every parent has a unique method of raising their children. Our mission is to make you aware of your children's perspective-why it is so important for them that you behave as their parent-coach. In this chapter, we present some actions you can undertake to help your children to become successful, as well as more specific ways this applies to the the success of the family as a whole and examples of entrepreneurs who were able to achieve success thanks to the guidance of their parents and coaches. If you understand your children's needs and implement this life model, both your child's life and your family unit experience positive change.

Parents and Coaches at the Same Time

The key question now is: What is a coach and how can a person become one? A coach is the person who teaches, reviews, guides, and accompanies a group or a person in a sport like a trainer. The coach is responsible for ensuring the performance and excellence of the person being coached. We believe that parents should become that. They should be the person who is beside their child, maximizing their potential, and accompanying them on the journey to reach their goals. Coaches share similar features regardless of the discipline or sport they train; in the same way, those who are parent-coaches display similar traits. These are some of the most important characteristics of a parent-coach:

- They have a positive mindset.
- They use positive terminology.
- They motivate their children with phrases like: You are a champion! You are going to win. You are the best. I know you can do it! Trust yourself.
- They give their child importance, such as spending time watching learning programs on television with their children instead of programs that would not benefit them.
- They learn and apply strategies to better raise their children.
- They admire and appreciate their child's actions.
- They seek and take action to guide their children towards accomplishing their goals.
- They never give up during the hard process of raising an entrepreneur.
- They take advantage of opportunities in their lives and their children's lives to teach life lessons to their children.
- They set a positive example.
- They learn from their children.
- They recognize their mistakes and learn from them.
- They routinely attempt to excel themselves and their

children as well.
- They establish order and discipline in a good way.
- They apply communication strategies towards a better relationship with their children.
- They love what they do.
- They are leaders.
- They are confidants and guides.
- They support for their children during difficult struggles, building trust and giving their children confidence.
- They make time to be available to their children, to listen, support, and accompany them.
- They provide their children with appropriate tools to succeed.
- The make good use of authority without abusing it.
- They are up-to-date on new technology and trends.
- They seek space for their children to develop their talents and skills.
- They are tolerant and educate with love.
- They are constantly monitoring and celebrating their children's progress.
- They work as a team with their family.

This list is a good outline of what a parent-coach does. Please determine which of these qualities you have and which ones you can improve upon. Take a few minutes to visualize how beneficial this could be for your child's development. It is important to understand these characteristics. Sometimes, the way a parent's love is expressed can be a detriment to their child's success. One of the most common cases we have observed is when the parents try to do everything for their children. They give them everything without letting them work to obtain the things they want or escalate the concept of giving attention to the children by removing their children's personal space or making decisions for them. A parent-coach is not a psychologist or consultant, much less a confessor. No matter how much you love your child or how much you want them to emerge unscathed from every difficult experience, "bite your tongue" as they say in Colombia. Let your child learn from life and make their own choices. Do not be the protagonist of your child's life story.

If you want to be parent-coaches, you must be aware of what your children like, then obtain as much information as possible on those topics. Look for opportunities for your child to develop their competence in these activities. For example, if your children love tennis, enroll them in tennis lessons, take them to the classes, support their training, encourage them at their matches, and put in the effort required to demonstrate you believe in their success.

If your child does not know yet what their passions are, it is important to provide them with different scenarios. They can gradually discover their talents, skills, and the activities that will attract their attention. You can create these opportunities through games, family programs, and fun activities. We have played at being doctors, architects, entrepreneurs, models, singers, actresses, and we have participated in many types of sports. We stayed updated in the advances of technology, which will be invaluable in the future.

Life offers multiple opportunities for people to excel at what they like. However, to excel in any field, you must participate in activities until you find the one. If you have already discovered your passion, it may be helpful to implement a number of different strategies that can help you achieve your goals. What better opportunity for your children to develop new activities than next to someone who loves them? When your child works towards achieving their goal, it is important to understand that you have an immediate role in his journey towards success. The parent-coach characteristics we displayed above can maximize the advantages your efforts provide.

Selena, Shakira, and the Williams Sisters

An excellent example of this subject is the Mexican singer Selena, an icon in the world of Latin music, who sang from an early age. Her father, Abraham Quintanilla, realized that his children had a future in the field of music. He decided to put together a musical band called "Selena y Los Dinos," in which Selena and her siblings played and sang. At first no one wanted to play, then they realized that they had talent for music. Their father guided them in everything, supported them, and sought out scenarios and gigs for them to perform at. From six years old, Selena sang with this band. As time passed, "Selena y Los Dinos" became more successful.

There came a time when Selena and her siblings had a resounding success, thanks to their talents, efforts and the support of their father. "Selena y Los Dinos" is a clear example of a father who knows how to be a parent and a coach. He discovered his children's talents, believed in them, and gradually led them to success and reach the goal of being famous.

Another good example is the case of the Colombian singer Shakira, one of the most celebrated women in the world, and her father. Shakira started singing when she was five years old. Her father, William Mebarak, detected a special "vibrato" in his daughter's voice. Mr. Mebarak fully believed in the talent of his small girl, especially after she composed her first song "Your Dark Glasses" (inspired by her father.) To this day, her father and coach has stood by his daughter every step of her career.

Shakira started in the city of Barranquilla, Colombia. She auditioned for her school choir, but was rejected. The director stated she "had a very high pitch and sang like a goat." The road was not easy for her, but William Mebarak always stood beside his daughter, motivating her to continue working to obtain her dreams. Mr. Mebarak had to make sacrifices in his life to provide the support his daughter's talent deserved. When she was just thirteen years old Shakira first signed with

Sony. She scheduled performances and her father unfailingly accompanied her to each stage. William Mebarak is a writer who devoted himself for some time to selling jewelry and very fine watches to raise his family. This man decided to leave his businesses and his life in Colombia to support his daughter's dream. The release of the album "Pies Descalzos" placed her high on the international ranking and was a total success. Shakira's talent became evident at that point. Without the support, company, motivation, and dedication of her father and coach, Shakira's career certainly would not be what it is today.

Now let's look at the example of the Williams sisters, recognized tennis players at the international level. Their parents, Richard Williams and Oracene Price, went beyond the traditional duties as parents to train their daughters from an early age. Mr. Williams always took his five daughters to the tennis courts, hoping that one of them would become a great player. Serena and Venus were more attracted to the sport and became dedicated to training with their parents.

The sisters focused on their tennis training instead of pursuing more carefree activities. They did all this because they wanted it that way, not because their parents forced them. They did it because they enjoyed practicing their sport. Many people came to believe that these sisters never enjoyed themselves, but did not realize their real fun was in playing tennis.

Thanks to the dedication, sacrifice, and effort of the girls and their parents-coaches, Serena and Venus started competing at an early age. Serena was four years old when she won her first tennis tournament. Before she was ten, she had participated in numerous tournaments and won most of them. All of this was possible because her father and coach supported her and provided a place to develop her talent.

In 2003, one of her older sisters died. Serena and Venus were both greatly affected by this tragic event. They did not allow grief to force them to give up their dreams. This was one of the biggest obstacles they had to overcome. As parents, you will also have to overcome difficulties.

After much work, Venus was ranked as the first and best tennis player. Because of the time and context in which they lived, their father did not send them to more tennis tournaments nationwide. He sought to protect his daughters from racism. Mr. Williams contacted Rick Macci, a well-known coach for his work with star athletes. Macci had the opportunity to observe Venus and Serena play when they were only nine and ten years old. At the beginning he was not so convinced of the girls' talent, but soon realized that they had an unstoppable desire to be the best in tennis. Macci gave them the opportunity to be part of his prestigious tennis school, located in Florida. As good parents-coaches, the Williams did not hesitate to move their family from California to West Palm Beach to continue supporting their daughters' efforts to play tennis.

We want you to understand the importance of being present with your children in the area they want to develop and accepting the activities that your children are passionate about. Being the parent-coach of your child is a very difficult task. As the parent-coach of your child, you will notice as your relationship improves and your child's confidence and communication skyrockets.

Today's parents do not realize that they can develop a friendship with their children, as long as in one way or another they are willing to become a child as well. Interact on their level and enjoy spending time with them. This is one of the best benefits of being a parent-coach. Our recommendations are based on our experiences. We know the benefits a child gains from having a supportive and understanding parent-coach. We urge you, from the perspective of all children, to recognize your words and actions have more importance in our lives than any other.

Finally, we are not telling you what to do. We are sharing experiences and recommendations that had worked for ourselves and other successful young people. Young people who excel, who have had an effect upon the world and become leaders in their professions, have had a coach or mentor by their side. The most effective coach is their parents because they truly believe in their children's talent and are willing to give their all for them. Start to be the parent-coach of your child. You will notice the difference between just parenting and parent-coaching.

Our Parents and Coaches

Our parents were our coaches throughout our lives, even while writing this book. They have always been there for us, supporting and motivating us. They have always encouraged us to meet our goals, no matter how large or small they were. They have always been there, whether we were confident of achieving our goals or afraid of the obstacles on the path to our goals.

Our parents and coaches have always been there in all our activities. When I (Stephanie) participated in soccer tournaments, my parents were my best fans. Before every match my dad taught me soccer tricks, like making passes and hitting with my head. The day of the game, they would go to support me and motivate me. They cheered for my team's win and encouraged us not to falter. It helped my friends and I play harder to become the champions of an important tournament in my city.

Maybe some of you are already parent-coaches for your children. Keep it up and congratulations on behalf of your children. We want to thank you for your amazing labor. For those who are not yet parent-coaches, it is never too late to start. Make the right decision and change your story today.

What We Expect

Sometimes kids think that parents, simply by virtue of being parents, know exactly what we think or how we feel. The mission of this book is to express to parents how your children and potential young entrepreneurs think, how they feel and what they expect from you. We are young people who grew up in the same era. It is likely they experience similar thoughts to our own. The three of us are young entrepreneurs with different personalities, learning styles, brain types, likes and dislikes, abilities, temperaments, and friends. We decided to use all these differences within our list of thoughts we had that which your children could also be thinking.

- Give us permission to go out with our friends.
- Go shopping for clothes with us and give us your opinion of how we look.
- Spend time with us, playing games and being at our level as young people so we can share more.
- Trust us.
- Choose to be our friends instead of going out whenever you have the opportunity.
- Tell us your problems. We want to help and support our parents.
- Listen and understand all the things that happen to us in school or with friends.
- Let us explain and support our ideas when we think different than you.
- Come home early for us to tell you everything we did during the day and to let us know what you did.
- Demonstrate that you care about us, not merely for us.
- Do not bribe us when you cannot make it to our practice or to a special event. (This is very common to happen unconsciously).
- Take time to go to the events in which we participate and to all the parent meetings at school.
- Pay attention to us.
- Support us in everything we decide to start on our own.
- Let us wear clothes we are comfortable in that make us feel confident.
- Let us learn about and explore using technologies such as the Internet, smartphones, tablets, computers, and robots.
- Do not punish or unconsciously offend us by saying negative things if we perform poorly in school.
- Let us live our own experiences and allow us to learn from

the mistakes we make.
- Give us the confidence to tell you our problems and do not use it against us when you are angry.
- Give importance to our dreams and help us to achieve them.
- Forgive us for when spoke rashly out of anger.
- Understand that we do not mean the cruel things we say.

These are just some of the expectations we have of our parents; it is likely that your children will have similar ones. Perhaps your children have additional ones, depending on their age and how they have been raised. We would like you to develop an idea of what young people expect from their relationship with their parents. It is important to understand this information and take these expectations into account when you interact with your children.

The Results of this Model in Us

We want to share the results we have achieved from several years of being young entrepreneurs. We have made many accomplishments, proving it is possible to fulfill dreams and achieve goals as a family. We think the best way to achieve goals is to ensure they are in harmony with the entire family's. Parent-coaches are the platform allowing their children to live without wasting skills. Children and young people need to develop their skills and talents as early as possible so that when they become adults, they can easily attain mastery over their desired skillset. An early start is the deciding factor between achieving and accepting.

Our parents made the decision to become parent-coaches

when we were very young. Since then, our parents have been eager to give us information, to explain the current problems of Colombia and the world. We made the decision to build our future at an early age. We have three siblings, which means we have different ideas, projects, and goals. They have supported each one individually and in the manner best suited to each child.

They have supported me (Karen) in the multiple sports I have practiced. This has helped me discover my talents, meet friends and develop my qualities that I did not know I have. They have supported my public speaking and my participation in Model United Nations, as well as in my active participation in the school student government. My dad always helps me write my speeches, and spends entire days listening to me repeat them until I get it right. Sometimes, I get tired, but that is when my father and coach is there to encourage me. This unconditional support has always been extremely important. When you have to give a lecture or a speech at an event to 1,500 people, and you are only eleven or thirteen years old, you must strive to meet the audience's expectations. I discovered that the public would always want to hear and achieve a different life, because if we can accomplish what we have, any person can.

My parent-coaches have always supported me; they were the ones who motivated me to study at a university outside of Colombia. They trusted me to decide to move to Atlanta, Georgia, in the United States to learn when I was only seventeen. Thanks to their support, I got involved in activities such as the international student organization, the Student

Government, Model United Nations, planning committees of the university, and being a member of an advisory board. After four years of college in Georgia, I graduated Summa Cum Laude with a degree in Psychology.

Additionally, I am a Practitioner and Master Practitioner licensed by Richard Bandler in NLP. I have been granted honors such as the best student in the Faculty of Psychology 2015, Golden Owl Awards: Award for Emerging Student Leader, Golden Owl Awards: Jerome Ratchford Award Student Leader, Who's Who Among American Students, the President's List, honorable mention for entrepreneurial excellence at Universidad San Martin in Bogotá, Colombia, Exaltation to the Entrepreneurial Merit in the Latin American Congress on Entrepreneurship in Panama, and the "Young Entrepreneur and Transformer" medal granted by the Junior International Chamber (JCI). The council of the city of Cartagena has declared me culture heritage. The above are just some of the things I, Karen, have been able to accomplish, because I learned to believe in my abilities due to the education I received from my parent-coaches. My accomplishments are not solely business-related. An entrepreneur knows to develop many aspects of their life. Regarding Chococar, we have opened Cookies and Cookies Laboratory a completely new concept in the market. We opened our first store in Cartagena, Colombia earlier this year. We have a clear vision-to make our brand an internationally recognized franchise. We are in the process of positioning our brand in the main cities of our country. We then plan to expand to other international markets.

At the moment, we continue writing books that will be released soon. In a few months, we will be launching a new book. We love to write and hope to contribute a grain of sand to the happiness and prosperity of families; it is definitely something that we will continue doing.

It would have been difficult to imagine that someday we were going to be hired by large multinational companies that would pay us to train their staff, or that thousands of people would buy tickets to attend one of our events in a country different from ours simply to listen to our message, or that so many people would buy our book. Today that is our reality, and it began with the effort our parent-coaches made for us to create a childhood business. All this has been possible because our parent-coaches have done their work in an exceptional manner. They prepared us, practiced with us, taught us public speaking techniques, investigated with us, and spent hours making sure that each of us succeeded at every event we attended.

The confidence to lecture and teach adults is just one of the skills that our parent-coaches helped us to develop from an early age. Chococar was an ideal platform for children, giving us the opportunity to acquire important values, get to know ourselves, and discover our talents, skills, and strengths. We received great benefits from Chococar and want your children to receive them, too.

Parents, we are not telling you that you have to do this; we are giving away a valuable strategy that works. This formula worked for our family. It has also been part of the effective formation of many successful world leaders. Try it out and see if it benefits your family. Please make the attempt-you will see for yourselves the difference between parenting and parent-coaching.

CHAPTER 6
NEUROLINGUSTIC PROGRAMMING: AN EFFECTIVE TOOL

"YOU SEE? YOU ARE ONLY GOOD AT DESTROYING THINGS, WATCH TV, AND EAT", "STUPID BOY, ALL YOU DO IS RUIN MY LIFE"

WEAK CHARACTER

LOW SELF ESTEEM

INSECURITY

One of the ways to become both a parent and a coach is to use practical tools to achieve the objectives proposed by the family. Neurolinguistic programming (NLP) is a powerful tool that has had excellent results in our family, which we believe can be truly useful for you, too.

We know about NLP because our father and coach began to study it many years ago. He became a Practitioner and later Master Practitioner. Our father used all sorts of NLP strategies to educate us. We learned these strategies by example, with exercises practiced daily at home.

Currently, I (Karen) am a Practitioner and Master Practitioner licensed by Richard Bandler, co-creator of NLP. My sisters Daniela and Stephanie are Practitioners and are studying to be Master Practitioners in this discipline. We plan to continue using, practicing, and learning about this topic because we have witnessed great results through its application in daily life.

The Americans Richard Bandler and John Grinder are the creators of this theory, which consists of practical strategies for communication, personal growth, behavior changing, beliefs, and goal setting. The essence of NLP is in the neurological connection that through verbal and non-verbal language can create specific programming at an unconscious level that has the ability to modify and establish desired behaviors.

The use of NLP in our entrepreneurship model allows human beings to have a greater control of our brain and mind in order to achieve the goals we set for ourselves. NLP is a tool for entrepreneurs to consciously turn daily experiences into learning scenarios, know ourselves better, improve our self-control, have a high self-esteem, and activate our skills to be successful. It gives parents many strategies to consciously program their children's minds in a positive manner and avoid making unconscious mistakes that can affect their children's lives negatively.

Our brain and an iceberg

Our brain is much like an iceberg, where only the tip of the structure can be seen above the surface, with the rest submerged under water. Our brain compares very well with this gigantic element, as its structure contains a conscious (aware) portion that only represents five percent of its total, and an unconscious part that consists of the remaining ninety-five percent of the brain.

We use these terms often in this book, and it is essential to understand the difference between these concepts and the important role that the unconscious plays in the life of all human beings. Additionally, this concept is one of the most important foundations of NLP and many of the strategies proposed in it. We have said that the unconscious mind is ninety-five percent of our brain, hence the large influence it has on the behavior of human beings, and the importance parents to learn to handle this concept perfectly to raise children to be winners and achievers in life.

The conscious mind is that section which we have total control over. With it we carry out functions such as reasoning, memory, perception, intuition, and imagination. Although these functions are very important, the unconscious mind is more important because thanks to it, we unconsciously perform physiological tasks that we consciously never learned to do and do not need to remember how to do them, such as breathing.

The unconscious mind is like a safe in which we store our habits, experiences, beliefs, values, and information that we collect throughout our lives. Our unconscious begins to collect information from the eighth week of pregnancy; even before birth our mind is already receiving information. Once we are born, we are like sponges that absorb everything we see, hear, and feel, regardless of whether this information can be good or bad for us. At that age we do not have the ability to discern, we are solely dedicated to absorbing and storing all the information that surrounds us.

The question then is: What happens to all that information we collect throughout our lives? That is the information we use to program our brains and shape our behavior. Imagine that your mind is like a computer, and the unconscious is the software that controls the tasks of this unit. As we know, computers do not think, they work according to the program that has been installed. Our mind also works based on the information stored in its unconscious.

The brain operates by recurrence, meaning it extracts information you have stored to react to situations that life presents. Let us apply this concept to a case very similar to one that your children can experience at school each day. Imagine that an eight-year-old is playing soccer with his classmates. Accidentally and unintentionally one of them stumbles and falls, making him fall to the floor as well. The child gets up off the floor and automatically gives a blow to the one who made him fall. He performs this reaction without even thinking, automatically or "unconsciously" he hits back.

Based on this situation, I want you to take a few minutes to think about the kind of programming that this child has in his unconscious. Most likely, the child in this example has been exposed to violence during much of his life, either witnessing fights or abuse between his parents, horseplay among older siblings, video games or television programs that show this kind of behaviors, etc. There is a long list of factors that may have influenced the aggressive behavior of this child. It should be noted that this aggressive behavior was acquired and molded based on the information he had accumulated since before birth. He acted in response by doing what he has seen, heard, or felt in his few years of life.

I hope that at this point, you are already realizing the importance of the unconscious in each person's success or failure. Your children are absorbing information that surrounds them every day. What is in the unconscious of your children?

This is where NLP plays an essential role. Through strategies you can CONSCIOUSLY program the unconscious minds of your children with every word, action, game, and life situation. Parents, you are still on time to review and reassess how you are working your children's minds. We want you to read this information with love so that you can implement NLP techniques, and program the "software" of your children's mind for them to be successful and prosperous early in life.

For the brain, thinking is the same as doing

Having explained what the unconscious mind is and the importance of it for each and every person, we will now talk about how to program the brain and some features that are important to know. It is clear that humans, from kids to adults, act by recurrence to information we have stored in our unconscious mind.

The first thing we want you to be clear on with reference to the brain is that to think about something is the same as doing it. It may sound confusing, but it is essential to understand that our brain generates the same emotions and physiological reactions when we have a thought about an action as it does when we are physically performing the action.

Practical Exercise

I will present an exercise to demonstrate that for the brain, thinking is the same as doing. Your mission is to read the following text, and imagine a clearly detailed, step by step picture of what the words say: Imagine a lemon. it is a very intense, dark green color. The lemon is hard because it is not yet ripe. You slice this lemon in half, and you realize that although it is not ripe, it is very juicy inside. When you split it in two, you feel the wet, sticky sensation of lemon juice dripping across your hands. You decide to take one half and bite it. When you do, you can taste the sour lemon, puckering your mouth.

Did this make your mouth water? Did you feel the sour taste of lemon as if you had really bitten into it? These reactions are the product of our brain that does not differentiate between thought and action. It is very important to consider this in our daily lives because we may be hurting and limiting ourselves doing things exclusively because of the thoughts we have about them.

Let's talk about phobias, intense fears toward something that in reality pose little or no risk or danger. Phobias tend to be constituted after the constant repetition of thoughts and images that the person plays and records in his/her mind about all the bad things that can happen if an action is done. Incredibly, one of the most common phobias in the world is the glossophobia, or fear of public speaking. Have you heard of someone who has died from having to speak in public? Probably not, and neither have we. Public speaking is not the problem; in fact, the best way to overcome this phobia is by speaking in public and proving to yourself that it's okay to do so.

Phobias

This phobia of public speaking starts when images of all the bad things that could happen are constantly repeated inside your head. In the case of a child, for example, he might imagine that his peers will make fun of him, that he will forget what he must say and run off, that he is going to faint, etc. When people begin to think about these things, the brain produces physiological reactions such as rapid heart rate, anxiety, sweating, or rapid breathing, among other symptoms.

We emphasize that is not necessary, in the case of glossophobia, to actually speak in public to experience all these symptoms. Just thinking of the idea of public speaking is enough for the brain to create these physiological reactions that we mentioned above. The same is true for all phobias. This is because, for the brain, thinking is the same as doing.

Use it at Home!

We established that for the brain to think is the same as to do. The key lies in learning how to use this information positively in your lives, especially at home with your children. Phobias and negative thoughts occur with respect to an action or object. Positive and motivating emotions can be produced in exactly the same way.

You can increase the level of self-esteem and motivation of your kids by making a practical exercise in which he will ask you to imagine and create clear images in his mind where he sees himself ending first place in a race, winning a baseball game, or simply reciting a poem at a school event in front of all the students. The idea is to help your child imagine how success feels, looks, and sounds in the activities in which they participate. The constant repetition of these images of happiness, accompanied by your words of encouragement, generate a burst of positive energy that will convince your child that he or she is able to achieve absolutely anything they sets their mind to.

Three Effective Techniques

To start applying NLP techniques, it is essential to have basic knowledge of the unconscious mind, as most of these techniques work directly with the unconscious mind. The following are three techniques that are particularly effective in improving issues such as communication, self-esteem, and achieving goals within your family. These techniques also have great applicability at work, in career relationships, and especially for personal growth.

1. Rapport

Rapport is one of the most basic tools that exist in NLP to develop an effective communication, allowing you to transmit your message and achieve the purpose of the conversation you started. Communication is absolutely essential in the work of a parent-coach. Let's recall that one of the major problems that occur between parents and adolescent children is lack of communication. Good management of verbal and nonverbal communication can lead to better relations with your children, while building a relationship of trust and happiness in the family.

We use rapport to unconsciously influence the person we are talking with to create a more fluid, comfortable connection with us. The main objective of this technique is to create synergy with the person with whom you are communicating in order to achieve a pleasant atmosphere of empathy, trust, and cooperation and allow a positive flow in the conversation.

There are times when we feel that as a whole group we are "speaking the same language." We feel we are all integrated, contributing to the conversation and actively listening to all the participants. In such situations, it can be said that a good level of rapport has been generated. There are also situations where some long, awkward silences happen in conversations where it is obvious that the participants have not developed this mental connection. Rapport is established unconsciously, and we want to show you how you, as parents, can CONSCIOUSLY generate high levels of rapport in the conversations that you have from now on. It should be noted that this technique can be used both with your children and in other settings.

How to Speak the Same Language and Dance to the Same Music

There is a long list of ways in which you can establish rapport with someone. We will describe 4 ways that are fairly easy to apply to people of all ages.

• Imitate Body Parts
This technique is to imitate and match movements that the person you are talking to does repetitively.
Example: If the person you are talking to blinks their eyes constantly and quickly, then you should match that person's blinking rate of speed and consistency.

• Vocal Qualities
In this mode, you should match shifts in tonality, tempo, volume, timbre and intonation.
Example: If the person you are talking to uses a soft and low tone of voice, try using your voice in the same or similar way.

• Verbal Qualities
In this case you must be very attentive to the tense that the person you are communicating with uses, and try to use the same tense as much as possible.
Example: If the person you are talking to is speaking in the future tense, you should also speak in the future tense.

• Repetitive phrases
Carefully listen to phrases or words that the other person repeats or uses frequently and include those exact phrases in the conversation.

Example: If you are talking to a person who repeatedly mentions the word "cool" to refer to something that is good, entertaining, or enjoyable, try using that same term in the conversation.

The aim of the above strategies is to consciously establish a mental connection or rapport. These methods should be done discreetly, without telling the person you are talking to. Once you start using these tools you have to be very cautious. Note that as you use them more often, you are going to start doing it unconsciously, almost automatically. Try it, evaluate the results, and start enjoying the benefits of effective communication.

2. Anchors

We've been talking about mental programming techniques. An extremely powerful method is known in NLP as anchoring. Basically, it is to generate an unconscious association between a stimulus and an emotional response. In simpler words, the anchors are mental programs that use a cue to activate a feeling or an emotion.

We have been anchored in different ways. Throughout our lives we have unknowingly been marked by our parents, teachers, grandparents, older siblings, friends, or even television commercials. A common example of an unconscious anchor is when we hear a specific song that makes us happy because we heard it at a moment of total happiness and automatically remember the mood we associate with it. The opposite can also happen. Perhaps specific song leads us into a bad temper mood or makes us sad because it reminds us of an unpleasant moment we lived.

Another example of anchors that are created inadvertently are perfumes. There are people who always use the same fragrance, and unconsciously we associate that scent with the person that uses it repeatedly. This type of anchor can be used intentionally to mark an identity. For example, our father and coach always uses the same cologne so that when he arrives at his office, he does not need to be announced at the door. The smell actually tells people he has arrived.

On a daily basis, we anchor and are anchored unconsciously. A person is anchored when he/she is screamed at, hit, insulted, mistreated, or when something is repeated continuously. A person is anchored when he/she is treated well, smiled at, given a symbol that is recognized as a good sign (thumbs up), hearing how good they are at something, or when they cause someone to laugh. Just as there are very positive anchors that can create positive impacts, negative anchors may create negative impacts on people.

Your children are exposed to anchors every day at an early age by their teachers, siblings, classmates, TV, and especially by their parents. It is very important to repeat that bad programming or negative anchors can cause serious effects on the self-esteem and character of your children.

Often situations arise in which parents are angry with their children. These situations make parents change the sweet words they usually address their children with for verbal and physical abuse that strongly marks them negatively. You may wonder why the insults in a moment of rage are able to program a child so severely, and the sweet words spoken most of the time do not generate the same result.

The answer is: for an anchor to be truly effective, it requires a "glue" that is an emotion. It can be happiness, anger, sadness, etc. Thus, the stronger the glue (emotion), the faster and stronger the anchor will be. For example, in a situation where a mother is scolding her son and he cries (emotion of sadness) because his mother telling him phrases such as: You are such a disappointment, Can't you do anything right? Are you really that dumb/slow/stupid/lazy? You should be ashamed of yourself, You ruin my life. This child is recording and saving this programing due to the very strong emotion that he feels: weeping and sadness. This is added to his mother's words, which makes him consider those statements as true.

You affect your children with love!

Parents, the above phrase is very common nowadays. With love, many parents are unconsciously negatively programming their children. It is time to realize that anger is not a reason to ruin your children's success. The words said impulsively are apparently forgotten, but they are preserved forever in your children's unconscious mind.

There are other cases where it is not the parents who program their children. For example, often the older siblings or even child's teachers are the ones who call them dumb or ignorant. Children can receive this negative programming three times a day, every day of the year. This programing is effective, but unfortunately its consequences can result in trauma, poor academic performance and a desire for them to quit challenges without even trying.

Use it at Home!

It is time that parents begin to correct the program settings recorded in the unconscious minds of children and start projecting them as entrepreneurs and leaders with great capacities. Creating positive anchors is a matter of choosing the words you want to record in your child's unconscious mind and using them in connection to a moment of extreme happiness.

First of all, choose the phrases that you want your child to anchor. We recommend phrases such as: You are a champion. You can do it! You are smart. You are excellent. You can accomplish whatever you set out to do. You will succeed. Believe in yourself! I will always support you. Any other motivational phrases are appropriate. It is important to use the same phrase repeatedly in order to create an effective anchor.

Find the right time to create the anchor. It must be one in which there is a strong emotion present, preferably happiness. For example, after taking your child to a park that he/she loves, after they obtain an achievement at school or completed a task you set for them. It is also important that from now on, at all costs avoid scolding your children in moments of anger or during strong feelings of sadness with offensive words. Remember that at this time, effective anchors are created and they will be negative for your child.

3. Clear Commands

The last Neuro Lingustic Programming technique that we want to share with you is how to give clear commands to yourself and your children. We say yourself because many people do not have the ability to give clear commands to their own minds. This is a potential obstacle to performing a desired action. Parents must learn how to give clear commands to their children.

By commands, we refer to orders or instructions that parents tend to give their children. We have had the opportunity to talk with several parents who tell us about their concern of "children not listening to them." After several sessions in which we analyzed this ongoing situation, we concluded that in many cases children ignore what their parents say because the instructions, orders, or commands are not given properly.

Orders and commands given by parents to children transcend beyond instructions for their children to be disciplined or to do a specific task. Clear commands are the key in establishing effective, feasible, and achievable goals, both in your own mind as well as in your children's minds. The first mistake by which people fail to accomplish their goals is that these goals were not registered in their mind because they were not installed correctly. There are important factors in mental programming that are used unconsciously by parents on a daily basis. Our mission is to show them to recognize these factors in order to use them for achieving a successful education for their children which will lead them to become entrepreneurs at an early age.

The Unconscious Rejects the Word "No"

You have probably heard many times how important it is to talk with positive terms and to avoid being negative. There is a lot of reasoning behind this. There is a legitimate explanation at the unconscious level. The unconscious does not process negatives and it absorbs pictures rather than words. If you say "I don't want to eat fast food," the unconscious generates a picture of you eating fast food. Switching that negative picture to positive could be a lot more beneficial. An example of this would be, "I want to eat healthy food." The word "no" is one of the factors with the biggest influence in the formulation of clear commands, and therefore in effective mental programming. This explains why many orders parents give to their children are not obeyed or complied fully.

Please picture the following scenario:

A four-year-old girl is very close to a hot iron that rests on the floor to cool. In order to prevent the girl from burning her hand, her dad immediately tells her, "Do not touch the iron." However, the girl puts her hand on the hot metal.

Now, please imagine this scenario:

A four-year-old girl is very close to a hot iron that rests on the floor to cool. In order to prevent the girl from burning her hand, her dad immediately tells her, "Stop and walk back over here." The girl stops and goes towards the direction given. What is the difference between these two commands, and why is the second one much more effective?

In the first case, a negative command is used and the girl's unconscious ignores the word "no," pictures herself touching the iron, which triggers the action of touching hot metal. In contrast, the second command is a clear and positive order of what the girl is supposed to do. As a parent, you do not want her to touch the iron, however, instead of telling this to the child, you show her a clear alternative of what she should do. Do you notice the difference? The rejection of negative commands by the unconscious is the reason why the brain doesn't properly assimilate the former examples. Children search in their unconscious for any previous information related to what they are about to do in order to take the best course of action. For example, if this kid has already been burnt by the iron, he is probably not going to touch it again. It is much more effective to directly provide children with clear and positive instructions that will lead them to do what you want them to do.

We hope you now understand why some apparently clear orders are actually confusing in a person's mind. Giving positive commands is the first thing you should consider when setting a goal with your children. The following are some of the most common negative commands used by parents:

- Do not be disorganized
- Do not be rude
- Do not scream
- Do not eat too much candy
- Do not play with that bike
- Do not sleep late
- Do not hit your brother/sister

The way we suggest to give the above commands would be:

- Be organized
- Be nice
- Use a gentle tone of voice
- Eat healthy
- Play with the ball
- Go to sleep early
- Treat your brother/sister with love

This chapter is one of those you should read two or three times. The large amount of information presented here is probably new for many. The best way to fully understand it is through repetition. We ask you to please receive this information with love. Science has helped us establish practical tools that can be used at home to raise a child with high self-esteem, confidence, and leadership. Our intention is that you exploit this fully, so that every word and moment with your children contributes positively to enable them to become successful entrepreneurs at an early age.

"GO FOR IT SON, WE SUPPORT YOU. YOU ARE VERY TALENTED, FOLLOW YOUR DREAMS"

HIGH SELF ESTEEM

HIGH SELF CONFIDENCE

CHAPTER 7
BELIEFS

**GO TO SCHOOL
GET A DEGREE
GET A GOOD JOB**

Our parents have always told us that we are born entrepreneurs. We take the initiative to crawl when we are babies. If we are all born entrepreneurs, then we should all have the same probabilities of being successful and happy. Then, why are some people rich and others poor? Why are there happy people and sad people? Why do some people prosper and other people always seem to stay the same? The real question then is: What makes the difference?

We have thought of different ways to answer this question. The time and experiences we have had and the studies we have completed led us to the best possible answer to this question: beliefs. Ladies and gentlemen, the beliefs each person has are responsible for leading the way to success or failure. Beliefs are the key determinants in the life of an entrepreneur. That is why we decided to place so much emphasis on them, so that you, as parents, can use them beneficially.

The concept of beliefs must be understood in a simple way. They are everything that each of us considers true. Absolutely every person has beliefs. They are required in order to live, since we use them to create our mental structures and act upon them. From the most basic actions we perform to the most complex, they are all based on our beliefs. For example, my mother drinks coffee in the morning because she believes that this awakens her. If my mother did not believe that coffee had the effect of giving her energy, she would probably opt for taking any other drink. This small example shows how a person makes choices and decisions based on their beliefs. It is imperative to understand that the most important decisions in a person's life are also grounded in the beliefs that they consider true.

Beliefs are necessary in everyone's life. Because of them we have the capacity to generalize our perceptions of the world and act. It may be a little difficult to identify all the times we act or make decisions based on our beliefs, because they are so common that they become unconscious actions. Below is a list of common beliefs:

- I study because it will help me have a better future
- I work hard because it brings rewards
- I do not steal because it is wrong to do so
- I do not waste food because it is unfair

- I treat people well because it is right

We give these basic examples to clarify the concept of beliefs. Now that it is clear that people act based on the beliefs that they have stored in their unconscious mind, the question is: What if the majority of the beliefs installed in a person's brain were all negative? Most likely, a person with negative beliefs would live frustrated due to their inability to take action to fulfill their dreams. They would probably not believe in themselves. They would be likely to waste opportunities. This is why it is truly important to learn how to manage our beliefs, as these can turn into one of the biggest obstacles or benefits in the road to becoming successful and happy!

When a belief becomes limiting it inhibits us mentally and physically from achieving our objectives. They turn into a false ceiling in our mind, preventing us from going beyond where we are at the moment. People perceive them as fear, terror, fright, and other negative feelings that will not let them take action. These limiting beliefs are also unconscious and difficult to recognize, hence the importance that after this chapter each one of you make a thorough analysis of the beliefs limiting your lives in one way or another. On the other hand, it is important to think what limiting beliefs are you teaching your children that are unconsciously negatively affecting them.

One of the peculiarities of the limiting beliefs that people create in their minds is that they tend to be based on unproven facts that are not true, or things that they have never tried, such as: I am not able. It is very difficult. I am too old. That's impossible. I'm not good at that. It takes too long to achieve.

It is only for women. Those are just a few of the most popular examples of the long list of beliefs that we have heard which limit people from being who they want to be. In the same way, one can have positive beliefs that act as an engine and motivator to achieve our goals and dreams. If I believe I can do it and I have everything it takes in order to succeed, I will probably act according to that belief.

Flea Circus

The flea circus became a popular attraction in England around 1830; it was attractive for people to watch fleas be the main performers of circus tricks. Incredibly, fleas, small animals known for their great ability to jump, could be trained and the process was quite simple. Dozens of fleas were introduced in containers with lids that will not allow them out. The fleas naturally jumped higher and tried to escape, but failed when they hit the top of the containers. After only two days of training, fleas learned to adapt their jumps to the height of the top of the container to avoid bumping against it. After this short training period, the cover could be removed, and the fleas kept the same height on their jumps and did not even attempt to escape.

What is more surprising is that when these fleas reproduced they taught their offspring to jump only to the height of the container's top, which was now imaginary. Fleas taught baby fleas this to prevent them from getting hurt. Little did they know that they were limiting the potential from generation to generation of new fleas.

Just like fleas, the nature of a parent is to protect the child at all costs. The example of the flea circus shows us that even with the good intention of wanting to protect them, they may be limiting their offspring's potential. Your life experiences as parents, are not necessarily the same as those of your children, which is why some of your beliefs may not apply in their lives.

The topic of beliefs is very broad and we would need many chapters to lead you through a comprehensive analysis on how to identify and remove the beliefs that limit each of you. For the purposes of this specific book we will focus on how your beliefs are unconsciously impacting the lives of your children.

How are beliefs formed?

We all come into the world with an empty hard drive. In other words, we are born with zero information in our unconscious mind. As we grow older, we experience situations that help us acquire information and make generalizations about the world. Although some of the beliefs we form are from experiences we have had, the largest source of beliefs are our parents.

From the eighth week of pregnancy on, babies have the ability to perceive information from the environment, especially from their mother. After birth, this ability becomes even greater, and although infants do not understand everything that happens around them, they are absorbing information from everything they hear and feel. At an early age, children are unable to distinguish whether the information they are receiving is harmful or beneficial. They simply absorb all this information and start building their perception of the world based on it.

Parents, teachers, grandparents, babysitters, older siblings, television, and the internet play a key role in the beliefs that children adopt. This chapter was written to make you to think about the type of information being recorded on your children's hard drive. Remember, they will act the rest of their lives based on the information stored there.

Beliefs and Entrepreneurial Children

We will focus on the beliefs and information being transmitted to your children related to their success, happiness, prosperity, and potential. After more than thirteen years of having decided to become entrepreneurs and listening to other entrepreneurs, we have realized that one of the biggest obstacles a child or young person who decides to be an entrepreneur faces is his parents. Unintentionally, they have beliefs and attitudes related to the time in which they were educated. We are not referring to beliefs related to values, education or manners. We are referring to beliefs related to productivity and the financial education of children.

Let us recall that beliefs are installed and are transmitted unconsciously. In other words, it is not necessary to tell a child a negative or positive belief literally for him/her to adopt it as true. Children look, listen, feel, and unconsciously learn from these elements. Based on them, they begin to create their perception of life. That is why all parents should be careful about the way they act with their children.

Anti-entrepreneurship Beliefs at an Early Age

Of all the beliefs that we have heard, there are two that are really anti-entrepreneurship:

1) Children and Young People Cannot Make Money at an Early Age

Many adults still have the belief that children and young people are not possessed of the capacity, should not, or cannot produce money. This belief may have been set in the minds of some adults for countless reasons. It is likely that children and young people who are around adults who have this mindset believe that they are unable or cannot produce money. As a result, these children and young people never even try since entrepreneurship is not even an option for them.

We are an example that shows that this belief is completely wrong. We sold chocolates door to door and generated profits from our sales before we were ten years old. Our parents always believed in us and led us to believe that it was possible to generate income from an early age. Thanks to that, we worked hard and grew our chocolate company, Chococar. After Chococar, we started other business activities. Today we continue to run our companies and decided to start down the investors path. We were able to do it because we always believed that we were capable and that running our business as kids was possible.

We are not the only example; there are many young people who have become millionaires before turning twenty-five.

Two years ago, we had the opportunity to meet David and Catherine Cook, two siblings who created MyYearbook.com. They started with an investment from David. This site is now valued at one hundred million dollars.

We propose changing the belief that entrepreneurship is for adults and we invite you to change this paradigm for a belief that will bring very successful results: the earlier you begin to do business, the better your results will be. In our opinion, there is no minimum age to become an entrepreneur. Your child could start a small business playing and having fun and gradually, it could become a lifestyle. Your child can grow with the belief that he can be a successful entrepreneur.

2) Study - Be Professional - Get a Job

One of the biggest problems faced by many countries is the high rates of unemployment. There are different hypotheses that attempt to explain the reasons and propose solutions to this problem. We believe that one of the factors that contribute to high rates of unemployment is the beliefs of a large part of the population. Children grow their entire life listening to their parents, their teachers, and their grandparents repeating the importance of studying, getting good grades, graduating, and then finding a good job.

The constant repetition of this idea creates a mindset that turns into a belief. Students basically spend all their lives studying to get a great job that is not always available. This is why we often see people working in different fields than the one they went to school for. The problem begins when they can't find their dream job. The chances that these young adults will become entrepreneurs are low because they never considered the entrepreneurship path or are already affected by the system.

We have met many parents who focus on their children to be completely academic, without considering that they may have other skills and abilities. These parents tend to force their children to be excellent in school. They do not offer them the opportunity to explore their talents or develop other non-academic activities. We are not suggesting that school is not important, but we are saying that it is even more important to have space to develop activities in order to discover abilities, skills, and talents. Sports, arts, or dance are alternative options for activities other than academic; nevertheless, we recommend entrepreneurship as the best option to discover and empower skills. Encouraging and guiding your child to start his business is an excellent pedagogical exercise where he or she will discover their abilities. This is the best way for your children to install the belief that it is possible to be young, successful entrepreneurs and erase the traditional belief of studying and getting a job.

We reiterate the importance of education, but focused on the development of financial intelligence and skills that can become a business or a productive activity. We encourage all parents to guide their children to start their financial life at an early age, so they can have an alternative path to follow and be successful.

Every day that goes by, we are more convinced that changing

and deleting the beliefs that limit us at a young age is the best investment you can make as parent to raise an entrepreneur. Since our parents decided to delete these limiting beliefs and motivate us to accomplish our goals, we have noticed that every day we feel more committed to our company, and every day the opportunity to learn becomes more attractive and interesting. School and college became interesting to us because knowledge became a priority. It is your chance to do it, and we guarantee you is worth it!

We have already shown several tools that can be used to become excellent parent-coaches for your children. Now we are going to introduce one that has had incredible results in our family: the triune brain. This theory has many uses in the world of education; however, we want to share it with you so that you understand yourselves as well as your children.

When we say understand, we are not simply referring to the type of food they like, what their favorite activities are, or what their best subject in school is. To understand your child surpasses them. We consider it one of the most important steps of being parent-coaches. By understand, we are referring to knowing the brain type of your child, knowing how they understand, comprehend, and learn, and knowing the most important features of their cerebral configuration.

When a family clearly comprehends one another's brain types, their relationships improve. You will have the ability as a parent-coach to avoid most conflicts and handle those that do arise in a strategic manner. Similarly, you will be a more effective parent-coach and deliver excellent results. In addition to focusing this theory on the family, we will also focus it towards developing entrepreneurship in your children from an early age.

Chapter 8
The Triune Brain

Waldemar De Gregori, a Brazilian researcher, is an adapter of the triune brain theory. According to De Gregori, our brain is a system that is composed of three parts or blocks: right, left and center. The left brain is mainly based on reason and logic and it learns more visually; in the right brain are the emotions and it learns by listening and intuiting; the central brain is the engine that sets in motion all these feelings and ideas and learns in a kinesthetic manner and by experience (by doing things.) In our book we refer to the three parts or blocks as the three brains.

All human beings have these three parts and their set of functions. We develop one of them more than the others, so we all have a dominant brain, one subdominant brain and a third brain. A person's dominant brain determines how they feel, think and react to a situation; the subdominant brain is involved in these processes, but to a lesser extent.

Following is a list of a number of features for each brain. As you read them, try to identify features that you possess, and the kind of brain that you feel more akin to. Then do the same for your spouse and children. The goal is to identify the brain types in your family by the end of this chapter.

Left Brain: Logic

- Analytical
- Rational
- Critical
- Supports arguments with numbers and statistics
- Specific
- Thoroughly communicates facts and events
- Verifies information before accepting it as true
- Perfectionist
- Plans activities in detail and evaluates their results
- Scans all options carefully before making a decision
- Writes well and uses words accurately
- Controls emotions
- Is a good interlocutor, always has a well-considered opinion
- Is anti-official, critic

Left brain types are logical, analytical, researchers, mathematicians, and calculating. They have a large vocabulary, think before acting, and are good with details. This brain learns more visually, by researching, and by memorizing.

Right Brain: Creativity

- Communicates easily with people
- Empathic
- Highly innovative
- Intuitive
- Responds with passion and romance to love, nature, and life
- Daydreams
- Impulsive
- Responds creatively to challenges and situations
- Conflict mediator
- Emotional
- Finds reasons to smile easily and enjoy life
- Very spiritual, feels a direct connection to a higher power
- Shows affection easily
- Sensitive
- Changeable

The right brain is creative, intuitive, innovative, impulsive, sentimental, pampered, religious, sensitive, and learns more by listening, intuiting, and meditating.

Central Brain: Action

- Is direct with people
- Knows how to take advantage of business
- Likes to make money
- Competitive
- Handy with electronic and mechanical equipment
- Organized

- Capable of repairing damaged items; is very good for manual labor
- Determined
- Wants immediate results
- Sets tasks, defines goals, and is precise when leading or giving directions
- Achieves goals despite any circumstances or obstacles
- Has a high sense of belonging
- Makes decisions based on a cost-benefit relationship
- Likes to take action and experience new things
- Takes risks
- Does not give up
- Likes to finish what they start

The central brain is where the following prevail: action, know-how, innate leadership, risks taking, meeting goals, sense of belonging, and aural learning.

After reading the characteristics of each of the brain types you may feel that you have the characteristics of several brains. This is completely normal and accurate. Everyone has three brains. We each have a dominant brain, a subdominant and a least developed third brain that interact to create the unique and unrepeatable way each person thinks.

Identify your type of brain accurately

The best way to accurately identify a brain type is by performing the triune ratio test. This test can be found in the appendix located in the back of this book, "How to identify your Brain and that of your Family." You can also take it online at www.parentsandcoaches.com You will find four different tests, one for adults, one for high school students, one for elementary school students, and another for preschoolers. These tests, which reveal your brain's characteristics, have instructions for how to take them. We recommend taking the test before proceeding further to be certain of your brain type. It will greatly assist in assimilating the remaining contents of the book.

How does each brain learn?

We have mentioned that right brains learn more by listening and intuiting, left brains learn more visually, and central brains learn more by experience. Be sure to fully understand these differences before proceeding. Lacking knowledge of your child's learning style can be a cause of disobedience, conflicts, misunderstandings, and delays in the learning process.
It is common to find parents unhappy with their child's grades in school. When analyzing the teaching style of most schools, we realize that traditional education is mainly designed for left brain types, who learn visually and memorizing. Where does that leave children who learn by listening or kinesthetic? These tend to be students who do not understand all of of the material presented during lectures; therefore, they have difficulties when studying, doing homework, or taking tests.

These situations also apply to the home. When parents do not know if their children are learning in a visual, auditory, or kinesthetic way, they can fail to communicate effectively with them. We have met many parents who are upset because they give apparently clear orders to their child, but their child does not do what they were told. The parents think that this child is disobedient or has behavioral issues. It is possible that the parent is not taking into account the child's comprehension method, and causing the communication rift.

Imagine the following scenario: Juan is giving his son an instruction. Instead of looking his father in the eyes, the child is looking the other way. Juan believes the child is not paying attention and says sharply, "Look at me, I'm talking to you." The child looks at his father, but at this moment the communication is cut off between the two because the child is a right brain type, so he learns predominantly by hearing.

If Juan had taken into account that his child is a right brain type, he would have understood that his child learns aurally and he could be paying attention without looking directly at his father. From the moment the child stares at Juan, he's making eye contact, but he does not really understand everything that his father is saying; therefore, the child carries out the order incorrectly. If Juan had learned that his son was a right brain type, rather than demanding that he look him in the eyes, he could have moved closer to his son and repeated the statement in a soft tone to catch and gain his attention.

Hopefully you are now aware of the importance of understanding your own and your family's brain types, as well as how useful it can be for improving relationships and better teaching your children. Now, we will describe some strategies for giving instructions and conveying an effective message to each person according to their brain type:

- **Left Brain (Visual):** For these folks it is a must to see, so parents should point to objects, places, people, show photos, videos, or pictures. Parents should help the child to imagine a picture or a situation in their mind so they know what it looks like. We also recommend using phrases like "From my point of view," "I see what you mean," and "I can imagine how it would look."

- **Central Brain (Kinesthetic)** It is necessary for them to feel. It is good for them to have objects in their hands when you talk to them, such as an anti-stress ball or a stuffed animal. It is important that you take them places instead of describing them, and that they can use their senses to feel textures, smell food, hear voices and noises. Use phrases like, "I feel that what you say is correct," or "I perceive what you say."

- **Right Brain (Auditory):** It is essential that these people can hear you comfortably. Use different tones of voice when giving directions. Approach them so they can easily hear your voice and repeat instructions to make sure they understand you. Use a strong tone when needed, but do not scream because it threatens their learning channel. Use phrases such as "That sounds good to me," "I'm listening," and "Have you heard what I am saying?"

We encourage you to use this information at home and at work and experience how communication and relationships improve and productivity increases.

Developing the brain with emphasis on entrepreneurship

As mentioned above, the theory of triune brain has numerous applications in the areas of: education, corporate development, and research, among others. We will focus on how this theory can be applied to develop entrepreneurship among children and young people from an early age.

Below is a chart summarizing activities that can increase the development of each part of the brain. The purpose of this chart is to practice activities to develop your child's subdominant and third brain. For example, if your child is right brain, then we recommend guiding him to develop the activities in the boxes corresponding to the left and central brain in order to work towards developing a more balanced proportion. It should be noted that the activities contained in the table are directed specifically toward entrepreneurship.

The studies we have done and the experiences we have had since we began our first company have established the great importance the central brain has in entrepreneurship. Remember, this part of the brain is where human action, a key component in entrepreneurship, is located. This is why it is essential to develop the central brain in children from an early age. If your child has a right brain type and likes to create, then teach him how to put his ideas into action. On the other hand, if your child has a left brain type and plans everything logically, teach him to carry out these plans through the use of the central brain.

	Triune Brain Applied to Entrepreneurship	
Left	**Central**	**Right**
Acquire new vocabulary (especially financial terminology)	Have a competitive spirit	Participate in dance, art and theater
Read and write	Be punctual	Stimulate the senses
Use more numbers in talks (prices, dates, percentages, etc.)	Learn more about the dynamics of money (prices, purchases, sales, savings)	Show affection to people
Always keep informed about international news	Make decisions, starting with the small ones (clothes to wear, food to eat, when to study)	Take time for spirituality
Manage technological devices such as computers, tablets, etc.	Pursue an activity constantly, develop discipline	Change the routine
Develop the ability to discuss with arguments	Take good care of their school supplies, toys, or possessions, foster a sense of belonging	Create inventions
Plan activities (keep an agenda)	Start a pedagogical company (to practice buying and selling)	Use more gestures - use hands and body language when talking
Encourage curiosity, ask many questions	Do manual tasks (cooking, sewing, fixing appliances, building)	Laugh and see the positive side of situations
Develop logic	Provide leadership among family, friends, classmates	Imagine how life will be in the future
Use critical thinking	Take initiative to start new tasks	Tell jokes

Brain plasticity allows our minds to change and adapt to different situations. Use this extraordinary feature to develop your own and your children's brains the way you want to. Parent-coaches can guide children to practice the activities according to the part of the brain that they want to develop.

We stress the importance of the central brain in raising an entrepreneur child.

To understand your children and to educate them according to their learning style and brain type are the keys to being parent-coaches. Besides improving communication in your family, you will be forming an entrepreneur boy or girl who will have the ability to activate his/her financial intelligence from an early age. It has definitely worked for our family and us. We are sure you will also receive wonderful results.

CHAPTER 9
THE FAMILY

Frequently, parents slip into thinking that their children should think, learn and act like their parents since they share physical or behavioral traits. This is a common mistake we see in families we have worked with. It is a serious mistake, since parents unknowingly force their children to be like them, regardless of whether their child has a totally different brain. These situations often cause conflicts, such as catastrophic fights, feelings of resentment, and even hatred in the family, with no apparent cause. Even worse, these situations can last a lifetime.

As mentioned above, truly knowing each member of the family is an excellent tool to avoid such situations. It also encourages a harmonious environment where parents and children can understand one another and communicate better, thus creating the best scenario for being a parent-coach. By knowing the brain type, how he/she learns and the behavioral traits of your child, you can develop a formula for your child to become a winner in his/her area of interest. Let us clarify the term "family" for the purposes of our book. We use the word family throughout our book, but by "family" we mean the nuclear family: father, mother, and children. Uncles and aunts, cousins, and grandparents will all be considered relatives. Only the children of the same mother and father are considered part of that family, not children of different parents. A clear comprehension of this term is required to understand this chapter's content.

At this point, you are already aware of your child's type of brain, and you know their learning style, as well as some of the features of their brain composition. In this section, we will conduct a deeper analysis allowing you to amplify your knowledge of your family. To understand this section you must be sure of the brain type you, your partner, and your children possess. If you have not done so already, go to the annexes of this book where you will find the Triune Quotient Revealer Test proposed by Waldemar de Gregori.

A Deep Family Analysis

Who looks like who? Trying to discover if your child is more like their dad or mom is a normal conundrum. Maybe the child resembles you physically, but behaves like your spouse. The child could have a physical resemblance to both, but does not act like either one. The real questions to be answered are: Which parent's brain did my child inherit? Whose behavioral traits does my child emulate? These questions may seem impossible to answer; however, we will guide you step by step. We will use our family as an example to explain each term, so you may easily apply it to your own.

There are two concepts that need to be clarified in order to perform this analysis. What do we mean when we say brain type? What counts as behavioral traits? By type of brain, we refer to the results yielded by the Triune Quotient Revealer Test proposed by Waldemar de Gregori, which determines if your dominant brain section is right, left, or central. The type of brain refers to the methods people use to think, process information, and act. On the other hand, the concept of behavioral traits refers to certain mannerisms and behaviors inherited from our parents such as gestures, gait, a specific type of laugh, and facial or body expressions. Although there are some behavioral traits that are extremely obvious, you may need a carefully detailed observation to identify others.

Our studies, including our work with hundreds of families and extensive research have shown that the majority of first born children (the oldest) is eighty percent likely to adopt the father's brain, the second born must take the brain of the other parent, or their mother's brain. In the event the first-born adopts their mother's brain, then the second child has to adopt their father's brain. Subsequent children may adapt the brain of their father, mother, older sibling, a parent's sibling, cousin, grandparent or even a close family friend who has had a strong effect upon the child during their formative years.

Behavioral traits are learned and assimilated from parents

from the time a child is in the womb. There is no specific discovery method to determine who has which parent's traits. Identifying them is not a difficult task, especially considering how obvious many of them are. Even people who are not family members quickly notice behavioral similarities. We can use our mother as an example. She and two of her brothers have exactly the same gait, the same laugh, and make the same gesture with their tongue when they concentrate. To help us identify behavioral traits, we must take another learned trait into account, a person's temperament. With this in mind, we can analyze factors such as anxiety, extroversion, responsibility, kindness, and neuroticism.

Kid	Behavioral Traits	Brain
#1	Mother	Father (Central Brain)
#2	Father	Mother (Left brain)
#3	Everyone	Chosen (Right brain)

Below you will find a chart with our family's brain types and behavioral traits as an example:

- Dad: Center-right-left brain
- Mom: Left-center-right brain
- Child #1 Karen: Center-right-left brain
- Child #2 Daniela: Left-center-right brain
- Child #3 Stephanie: Right-center-left brain

Daniela and our mother have the same kind of dominant brain; both are left, they are logical, analytical, numerical, visual, and think the same way. If we observe them together, they seem quite different at first glance. Daniela likes jokes, she is cheerful, and her dominant gestures are totally different from our mother's. Even though Daniela shares a brain type with our mom, she has the behavioral traits of our dad; her gestures and temperament are those of our father.

My mom and I (Karen) have exactly the same behavioral traits, both are calm, sensitive, and express ourselves using the same facial expressions. However, my dad and I are central brain types; both are leaders, operational, and achieve our goals no matter what. Stephanie has a right brain type; no one else in the family is right brain, which indicates that she probably adopted her brain from a non-family member. Stephanie can be observed as a mixture of behavioral traits of the entire family, and individual traits can be identified as taken from our parents and her siblings.

The following chart summarizes the same information presented above in a different format:

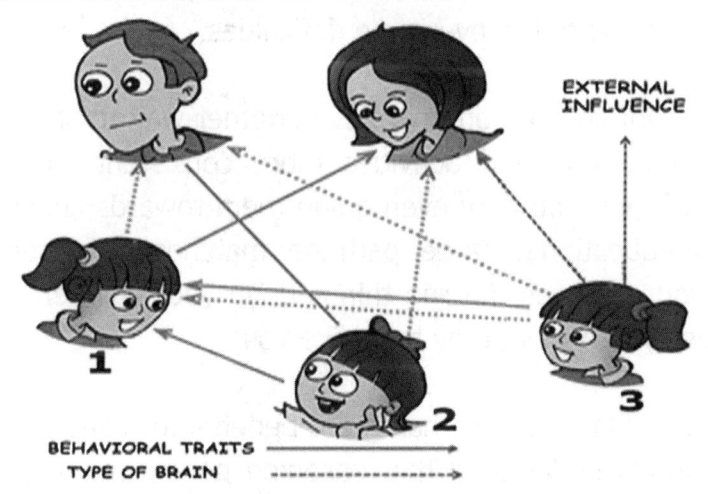

EXTERNAL INFLUENCE

1

2

3

BEHAVIORAL TRAITS
TYPE OF BRAIN

Perhaps you are suddenly realizing some things about your family. Maybe you understand why your child is different from you. He/she does not contradict you deliberately or randomly. Their brain type is different from yours. You now know that even if your child is physically similar to you, he/she might have the brain of their mother or father (or a different family member, or perhaps a family friend). That is why your child does not act exactly like you. Perhaps these situations were frustrating for you before, but now you know the reason behind their behavior. You have the capacity to understand them and use this knowledge strategically to influence your interactions. The most important thing is that you use this tool on a daily basis to train your children according to their specific personality.

In a family, there will always be two or more people with the same brain that think and act in a similar manner. If the family is not aware of this information, problems can arise. It can cause collisions in relationships or lead to an unconscious competition. Therefore, families need to examine this issue so they are prepared to overcome difficulties.

As a parent-coach, you now have another way to show your children options and activities more consistent with their type of brain. You may even guide them towards choosing a college education or career path that matches their strengths. Now you can avoid forcing things upon your children simply because you believe they think like you.

This particular tool also has great benefits for couples. Once our parents understood the reasoning behind many of their actions, their communication improved significantly. In addition, they have learned to interact based on their brain type. Our father's type is central brain. He achieves his goals no matter what obstacles come in the way, and he prefers to take action quickly. Our mother has a left brain type. She cannot act or make a decision without first examining all possible consequences. Before they started using these tools, my parents' difference in brain type caused many arguments. Now they better understand one another, have discussions with consideration for the other's brain type, and make smarter decisions.

Entrepreneurship in the brain

As always, we focus all these magnificent tools on the development of the entrepreneurial spirit of your children. The triune brain is particularly effective in achieving this purpose. It reveals important characteristics about entrepreneurship. It also allows us to identify which part of the brain should be developed to boost entrepreneurial competencies in your children.

The entrepreneurial traits are located in the central part of the brain. This is where human beings' actions are located. These are essential components which provide us with the ability to take risks, particularly those dealing with economy. If your child possesses the right brain type, he/she is highly creative, innovative, and has good ideas. They must develop the central brain so they can transform these ideas into realities. On the other hand, if your child has a left brain type, they are logical, scholarly, interested in research, perfectionists, and they often devise structured plans to develop the central brain so these plans can be put into action. This does not mean all central brain types are successful entrepreneurs. For those of us who have central brain types, we must develop the left brain to be more logical and analytical in our decisions and the right brain to be more innovative and creative in our problem solving.

We work to develop the central brain in people. This should be the dominant or subdominant brain. In cases where this is not so, we recommend you implement techniques to develop this hemisphere of the brain. Some of these basic techniques can be found in chapter eight. It is essential that entrepreneurs have a high level of central brain activity; otherwise, we would not have the ability to take risks. It is worth nothing that our brain has the ability to develop one section more than another as we work. For the purpose of being a successful entrepreneur, it is necessary to increase the level of the central brain.

When the central brain is not first or second in the configuration of an individual's brain, knowledge and imagination will be present, but they will lack desire for accomplishments and be unlikely to put their ideas into action. For example, a right-left-central brain person has the capacity to produce an innovative business idea which could be quite successful. After creating the business idea with the right brain, the subdominant (left) brain acts logically, analyzing the rationality and attempt to perfect the idea. They are unlikely to follow through on their ideas with actions. The opposite can also occur, in which a left-right-center person has the ability to develop an idea logically and rationally using their left brain, then his subdominant brain (right) acts based on emotions and starts generating conflicts which cause feelings of dissatisfaction with the concept and their surroundings.

It is possible for people who do not have a dominant or subdominant central brain to be successful entrepreneurs, but it would be much easier for them if they activated their central brain from an early age with the guidance of their parent-coaches. It is possible to develop entrepreneurship at home from an early age. Parents have a responsibility and great influence in this matter. It may seem a bit mechanical at first, to attempt to develop one part of the brain more than the other, but it will soon become a natural part of daily life.

The fundamental key to a successful family

In our concept, success is achieved after mixing some key ingredients. Family is on the list of the essential ingredients in the recipe. Remember that your child will unconsciously learn from everything they see, hears, and feel, even prior to birth. A happy, loving environment contributes to the entrepreneurial spirit of your child, and therefore to their future success. We give you these tools to make your family an indestructible block of love, understanding, and happiness working towards the same objective. The key is to put them into practice every day and turn them into a lifestyle to educate and train your children according to their brain type. It is up to you to adapt this system at home and help your children become achievers immediately!

CHAPTER 10
THE INFLUENCE OF MEDIA, FRIEND AND SCHOOL ON A YOUNG ENTREPRENEUR

A young person's environment plays a key role in their future life as a potential entrepreneur. Everything around us influences the way we think and the choices we make. Below, we will discuss the strongest environmental influences experienced by today's youth.

The influence of the media and social networks

These days, many young people spend much of their time doing sedentary activities. According to research conducted by Common Sense Media in the United States, adolescents (ages thirteen to eighteen) spend about nine hours using some form of entertainment media. Preteens (eight to twelve year olds) average six hours. This is in addition to time spent in school or doing homework. These activities include being in front of a screen, whether it is their phone, the television, computer, video game console, or tablet. Excessive screen time prevents children and adolescents from discovering and developing their talents. The most common cause of excessive electronic use is a lack of other activities to fill their free time. The Neuro Linguistic Programming training we attended states that these habits are part of a person's comfort zone, an area that prevents people from generating new commitments or setting goals.

Let us analyze television. On a daily basis we see many programs, including news broadcasts, focus on violence, tragedy, poverty, unemployment, injustice and other quite negative aspects. These programs affect our unconscious and impact on our attitude. Young people tend to unconsciously imitate behaviors seen in television programs. What we see is more important than what we think.

Like many other people our age, the authors enjoy leisure time. However, we understand that time is precious. We know we can use it for more productive things. Step by step, we have found a balance where we can spend more time on activities that obtain greater benefits and satisfaction. The key is to find activities one enjoys. We relish writing, lecturing, and leading companies. We realized that all the hours of television, Netflix, social networking or sleeping all day long were not going to take us very far. Sometimes, the desire to stay in bed and do nothing felt almost inevitable, but the motivation to fulfill our goals was more powerful. If there isn't a goal or purpose for a person to get up each day, it becomes more difficult to move away from lethargy.

All coins have two sides, including the influence of social networking and media in the life of an entrepreneur. Social media engines like Facebook, Instagram, Twitter, or Snapchat can become your best friend or your worst enemy. Many young entrepreneurs are extremely successful thanks to social networking. They use them to their advantage and generate profits through them. We live in a globalized world full of opportunities for smart people who choose to take advantage of them. The Internet is a great method for doing business and learning. It is an individual's choice whether they use social media or allow it to use them. Technology can be used to our advantage- it can help us organize and spur productive thinking. Every day, there is another app offering more benefits for a company or a new path to personal success.

Teens and preteens dislike having rules imposed on them. Everyone goes through this period of rebellion desiring autonomy, independence, and freedom. There is no absolute truth or magic recipe, but this is how our parents responded to our rebellious stage. Today, we thank them for it. We had established good communication habits and mutual respect, which made everything easier. Rather than simply allowing us to be on the computer all day or forcing other activities upon us, they gave us multiple options that would attract our attention. Trying to isolate a child or young person from technology today is practically impossible. Going out on family weekends, hiking, playing sports, or learning a musical instrument are good methods for replacing sedentary activity without making it seem like a punishment. Large amounts of money are not necessary, just the effort to create synergy with your child.

Use this new era's resources in their favor. Instead of banning television, show your children the positive side of the television. When we say the positive side, we are referring to all the programs that can inspire a child, such as films and programs regarding entrepreneurship, intelligence, music, cooking, art, or travel. Some of our favorite movies have an underlying message and have taught us strategy, communication or encouraged us to pursue our dreams. Television, used wisely, can be an excellent way to spend more time with your children. Be selective in what you choose to share with them; you can use television to send any message you want, but your children will learn from it.

The influence of friends

It is quite common for a group of friends to display the same type of behavior and have similar goals. Children sometimes do not understand the significance friendships have, but as they grow they start realizing that everything in the world happens through connections. Our father told us from early childhood that having the right connections can be the key to success. He was right! Today we have enjoyed many benefits from networking. You can convey this valuable lesson to your children. We guarantee they will thank you in the future.

As we grew up, we realized that friends from school and college play an important role in your life. The people you grow up with strongly influence the habits and behaviors you adopt. Our mother always said, "Anyone who runs with wolves ends up howling." Friendships can function as an engine that boosts us or as an anchor preventing advancement. There are "toxic agents" who will tell you that you cannot do something, that you are not capable, or they will simply mock your efforts. You may encounter people who do not believe in you. The main reason this happens is because these "toxic agents" do not believe in their own success. They do not want you to succeed and leave them alone. It is important that you and your child are able to identify this type of person.

Sometimes, people become envious and attempt to place obstacles on the path, rather than encouragement. It is very likely that most of your child's friends are not entrepreneurs and find it hard to understand what he or she is going through. The decision to become an entrepreneur comes with many sacrifices. As we worked, our friends were on the beach, at a party, or sleeping late. It is common to be judged and even teased by friends. This is where our character and intelligence had to make their appearance. We do not regret the choices we made. Today, we can see how fruitful our sacrifices were.

There are also friends who support you with the encouragement you need. A young person's interaction with positive-minded people or entrepreneurs is instrumental in the process of creating a business. To be surrounded by people who have a purpose in life, who have dreams and aspirations, helps set children on the path to entrepreneurship. We were inspired to become better every day by having friends with similar mindsets. Those friends are happy about our achievements and motivate us with their positive energy. The ability to interact and socialize is an entrepreneurial characteristic. There is an old saying, "In business, what counts is not what you know but who you know." We are positive of its truth today. In the world of entrepreneurship, positive friendships bring you closer and closer to achieving your goals. Surround yourself with friends who have the same vision as you, and your children will do likewise.

Friendships can influence the way to success for an entrepreneur, but one must develop a solid character to handle any type of person present along the way. Entrepreneurs have the ability to relate to all kinds of people without allowing them to affect or divert our journey. Nurture this quality in your children from an early age. They will eventually develop the ability to surround themselves with useful people, especially those who will contribute to their personal growth, without succumbing to negative influence.

The influence of school

School is an extremely important component in human life. According to the OECD report, children in primary school spend an average of 943 hours a year in school. For high school students, the number is even higher. At school we grow and transform from children to pre-teens to teenagers. During these twelve years or more, we learn more than mathematics, physics and chemistry; we learn values and behaviors. We store everything we see, hear, and feel in our unconscious mind for immediate or future use.

Parents do everything possible to ensure that their children have an excellent academic performance, but only a small percentage of a class achieves outstanding school performance. Countless times we are asked, "Why is my child not doing well in school?" The answer is, most schools do not know the brain composition of their students and do not understand how they learn. We can say that the educational system is "struggling against the current."

Usually eighty percent of students in a classroom are right brain dominant. They are intuitive, innovative, creative, impulsive, emotional and aural learners. Fifteen percent are central brain dominant. These are the leaders, persistent, achievers, risk takers, and kinesthetic learners. Only five percent are left brain dominant. These people are your researchers, scientists, perfectionists, mathematicians, and visual learners. Most classes are designed for left brain students: logical, rational, analytical students and scholars.

Imagine a traditional class: the teacher lectures for a long period of time and writes notes on the board. The students copy the notes, memorize the key information, and then take a test. It is disquieting to think that schools target only percent of their students! It is entirely possible your child a member of the other ninety-five percent of brain types the educational system is ignoring. This can explain why children find classes uninteresting. The material is intriguing, but the delivery is lacking.

In addition to identifying students, schools should impart a comprehensive, trichotomous education aimed at all types of brain. The topic of the triune brain in education is a seriously complex issue. However, it is important to understand the situation that your children go through at school, in order to provide the adequate support that he or she really needs.

Another reason why your child may not do well academically in school is because he or she can have other strengths and talents that may be ignored. Parents and schools often focus solely on a student's academic skills and forget that a young person may be the best dancer, singer, athlete, musician, or entrepreneur. Multiple investigations today have concluded that motivated children tend to have higher grades in school. If your child has lost interest in their studies, it is time to look for something that piques their interest, then support him or her in developing this activity to transmit that motivation to school. All human actions are caused by an impulse or motivation. Create a reward system by which achieving school goals will have a special value for your child. We can guarantee this will give better results than to force studying for the sake of studying.

School, a great opportunity for a young entrepreneur

The public education system is not designed to educate students on the topic of finance. It certainly will not teach them how to build a company. However, many opportunities occur daily at school that can develop their personal skills. One must identify these areas and take advantage of them. Most schools offer extracurricular activities, clubs, and events that can indirectly be converted into a business school. These scenarios are excellent ways to acquire entrepreneurial characteristics. We enjoyed school by assuming leadership roles. Through our school experiences we learned tenacity, respect, honesty, tolerance, organization and especially teamwork. Make the best use of resources available to develop leadership in your child-school is one of them.

When Daniela was in school, she sold brownies every morning before going to class. Selling at school was forbidden. The only way to sell things was through the school cafeteria, but the problem was that the brownies did not sell as quickly at recess as in the morning. Therefore, it was up to Daniela to create ways of selling without the teachers noticing. Once she was caught and suspended for two days. She knew she could not be suspended again, but neither could she afford not to earn the money. She sat down to negotiate with the school coordinator and created an association of vendors. The members of this association could sell their products before going to class and during class changes, and the school would receive a percentage of sales. After delivering a speech in support of her idea, and even providing a petition that had collected many signatures, the school agreed and the association was launched. Daniela was the president of the association.

Karen participated in organizing all kinds of events, from a model United Nations up to a national convention of ATVs. In the latter event she was responsible for ensuring none of the participants or attendees had an accident. She had to investigate safety standards and methods for preventing accidents. As a fifteen-year-old, she had to interact with adults, strangers, and manage a professional and appropriate language. In addition, she had to ask permission from the government to allow them to prevent a promotional caravan across the city. In all these events, Karen learned to work under pressure and make wise decisions at critical moments.

I (Stephanie) also organized intramural school sports and activities such as "Just Dance for Coexistence." The latter is a macro event I led when I was in ninth grade, where I learned the true value of perseverance and the importance of good leadership in a team. The idea of the event was to get many people to gather in one place and dance at the same time for one purpose: to promote conviviality. In addition to being the team leader, I was the singer of the song that more than a thousand people danced at the event. The months before the event were full of hard work. I had to promote the event, visit other schools and universities to teach the choreography. We struck a deal with the most popular radio station in the city, which practically guaranteed the event's success. It also taught me the importance of strategic alliances.

With these examples we want to show you that school can become an excellent venue to learn values and lessons for the future. To take full advantage of school, it is important to accept that academic achievement is important but does not have to be the sole focus of their development. Allow your child to take advantage of every opportunity to cultivate their skills and discover their talents.

CHAPTER 11
FINANCIAL EDUCATION

The type of education received by children at school is one of the most influential factors on the mentality they adopt when they join the workforce. At school and college, we are educated to become employees. This is not necessarily bad, but these educational institutions only show us one side of the coin. Many schools and parents insist on educating children in the same manner they were taught. Unfortunately, children do not respond well to outdated lessons.

The new generation is being educated upon old beliefs that no longer apply to today's world. From their first day at school, children learn they must go to school, get good grades, go to college, graduate with honors, and only then will they get a good job. Long ago, this may have been an effective path to a financially successful life. Today, many things have changed. The good jobs are few and hard to find. People spend twenty years or more preparing for the dream job, but once they enter the workforce, they encounter a reality they are unprepared for. Remember, the world has a lot of work to be done, but not many jobs to offer. Our society needs job creators rather than job seekers.

We want parents to understand how crucial it is for children to receive financial education. This will provide smart financial decision-making skills. Your children's mission should not be merely how to get a source of income, but to know how to manage, save, and invest their income. Our financial intelligence is developed based on our experiences. Children learn by example and repetition that is why everything that we live at home becomes a determining factor for our future actions.

Financial Homeschooling

In our family, money was never a taboo subject. Our parents talked to us about how to properly earn and manage money. Mom and Dad taught us that if we wanted something, we had to work for it. We understood that it was not possible to have everything we wanted instantly. We had to wait until we saved enough money to buy what we wanted or give something in exchange to get it. Our parents guided us in goal-setting, such as wanting a new toy, and in the process of earning and saving money to buy it. At home there was a reward system that allowed us to earn money in exchange for doing chores or having positive behaviors and achievements. While many of our peers were given allowances, we had to earn ours. Our parents paid us for chores and personal achievements such as scoring in a soccer game, or getting good grades. The system motivated us to behave well, but helped us understand the value of money.

Additionally, our parents taught us the concept of saving. Each of us had a piggy bank. At the end of the year we opened the piggy bank, and we divided the money into four accounts: one for savings, one for investment, one for spending, and one for sharing. Initially, our favorite was spending, but eventually we understood that the more the investment account grew, the more and better things we could buy in the future. We also understood how valuable generosity is; something as simple as buying candy for someone who had a bad day meant getting a big smile and making somebody happy. We also learned to take ten percent of the total amount we made and put it in our savings account. This whole process motivated us to continue increasing the total amount.

Each time we went out became an opportunity to learn how the real world of finance worked. When we went grocery shopping, our parents explained to us how to choose between two products, which price was lower or which product had higher quantity. They also showed us how discounts and promotions worked and how to take advantage of them. Sometimes they allowed us to choose what product to buy, or they gave us a set amount of money to buy a particular list of products. They also gave us money to pay the bill at restaurants or at clothing stores. Other times we played a game that was about adding up the three digits of the license plates or being the first one to calculate a percentage. Dad always says that everything in life is based on percentages. By the time we had to learn adding, subtracting and calculating percentages in school we were already experts.

Over the years, our goals became larger, with higher value. This taught us to think long-term, developed our vision, enabled us to plan ahead, and allowed us to fully comprehend opportunity costs. When Daniela was ten, her goal was to buy Barbie's car. For nine months, she stopped buying candy and small toys to save enough money. My parents explained that when selecting a major goal (in this case buying Barbie's car) one has to give up other alternatives (toys or candy.) These things she gave up and did not purchase were the opportunity costs of her decision.

Nowadays, when we make a financial decision we consider the opportunity cost and evaluate whether the cost is worth it. The term was invented by Friedrich von Wieser, and that many of our country's economic decisions are based on it. Knowing the importance of opportunity cost enabled us to make smarter decisions. As children, these decisions were of utmost importance. If we have one dollar, should it be spent on a cookie or ice cream? Performing this exercise as a child helps us weigh benefits and profits today. The concept applies to our companies and personal lives.

Another focus of our financial homeschooling was the importance of managing money. Many people have had a lot of money at some point in their lives, and years later they have nothing. Consider how many lottery winners end up bankrupt, or people who consistently have debt problems despite having a steady income. After a year of putting money in our piggy banks, investments had grown significantly, and we were contemplating what to do with the money. Our father always told us stories about his youth and how he had progressed from working at his farm in the countryside to becoming a successful entrepreneur.

He bought broken gold, waited until he had a significant amount, then when the price raised enough to make a profit, he sold it. After having saved for two years, the price of gold was at its peak, and my father sold everything he had to buy his first piece of land. One day, Daniela told our father she wanted to do what he had done. She wanted to buy gold, and needed him to guide me through the process. He was pleased to help. He explained that there are two rules that apply to any investment. The first is to have enough information, and the second is to buy at a low price but sell at a high price. Two years later the story repeated, but now Daniela was the one selling broken gold she had patiently saved.

Our companies, more than just being businesses, became a great source of learning and turned into in a true life school. Over the years, Chococar continued to grow and Quality Line did likewise. Usually people learn theory first and then practice; we learned theory while practicing. A pedagogical business can be an excellent way to financially educate your child. Our own experiences with it proved to be an effective learning method, and of course extremely fun.

Financial Education with A Financial Guru: Robert Kiyosaki

One day, our parents gave us an unconventional gift, the book Rich Dad, Poor Dad by Robert Kiyosaki. To be honest, we were not very excited when we received this gift. Reading was not our favorite hobby. Today, we can say that this was one of the best gifts we ever received. Next we will explain the most valuable lessons and the interpretation of everything learned from Mr. Kiyosaki and his great books.

Financial IQ

Robert Kiyosaki highlighted in several of his books the importance of increasing your financial IQ. Financial IQ does not mean how much money you earn, but how much money you have and how much that money works for you. In addition, it gives you the opportunity to know how productive you have been over the course of your life. To boost your financial IQ, you must increase your happiness, health, and freedom. Some people might get richer over time, but that money could make them less free due to the increased responsibilities, heightened stress or extra bills, and this could lower their happiness. In this case, despite having more money, their financial IQ would decrease.

Let's get a little more technical and calculate a financial IQ, according to Robert Kiyosaki, in different scenarios. Let's start by calculating the financial IQ of a conventional twelve-year-old child. There are two crucial concepts to this theory. The first is the mental age or the age indicating the financial intellectual development of the person and the second one is the chronological age or the physical age of the person. A person with a normal financial intelligence should have the same mental and chronological age, while a person with a higher financial intelligence would have a higher mental age compared to their chronological age. Conversely, if the person has a lower mental age than his chronological age it would indicate a lower financial intelligence. Now we will perform several exercises to calculate different financial IQs. The formula for financial IQ is mental age divided by chronological age multiplied by one hundred.

$$\frac{\text{Mental Age}}{\text{Chronological Age}} \times 100 = \text{Financial IQ}$$

Example #1 Twelve-year-old child:

1. Think of a twelve-year-old child you know.
2. Review the activities a child at this age normally does. For example: eat, play, watch TV, do homework, and go to school.
3. Identify the mental age of the child. To do this, assess whether the child you are thinking of has the ability to perform tasks for a child her age. If the answer is yes, the mental age corresponds to twelve.
4. Divide the mental age (12) by the chronological age (12.) Twelve divided by twelve is equal to one (12/12 = 1.)
5. Multiply the result of the previous division by one hundred to get the financial IQ. In this case 1x100=100. The financial IQ of the child identified is 100. This child is normal in our society.

Example #2 Forty-year-old employee:

1. Think of an employee who is forty years old.
2. Review the activities a person normally does at this age. For example: receives a paycheck, pays off his house loan, takes care of the car payments, pays for utilities and other expenses. The money does not work for him and he does not own his time.
3. Identify the mental age of this person. Evaluate whether this person has the ability to do the normal things that a person his/her age will do. If the answer is yes, the mental age is forty.
4. Divide the mental age (40) by the chronological age or real age (40). Forty divided by forty equals one (40/40 = 1.)
5. Multiply the result of the previous division by one hundred to get the financial IQ. In this case it is 1x100=100. The financial IQ of the person identified is 100, which is normal.

Now, there is a red flag in this case if we analyze it in depth. Suppose this worker continues to do the same things over a period of ten years. This means that his mental age would remain 40, but his chronological age would increase. Consider the following table:

	2010	2011	2012	2013	2014	2015	2016	2017	2018	2019
Mental Age	40	40	40	40	40	40	40	40	40	40
Chronological Age	40	41	42	43	44	45	46	47	48	49
Financial IQ	100%	97%	95%	93%	90%	88%	86%	85%	83%	81%

Most conventional workers do the same things over and over for many years. They do not change their routine, their way of producing income, nor do they reinvest their money or progress financially. Often, they are caught up in what Robert Kiyosaki describes as the rat race. This situation is distressing because every year their financial IQ lowers and so does their level of productivity.

Example #3 Entrepreneur Children

1. Identify a child entrepreneur. For this exercise, we will take our twelve-year-old selves as an example.
2. Review the activities a child this age normally does. For example: eat, play, watch TV, do homework, and go to school.
3. Identify the mental age of this entrepreneur. We must evaluate the activities we participated in and skills we had at twelve. At this age, we did many of the same things as any other child of our age, but we also had two companies producing a monthly income. We traveled internationally lecturing on entrepreneurship. We spoke with a fairly advanced business vocabulary, we read articles of general interest and we received financial education. We led a nonprofit organization that fostered entrepreneurship among young people of limited resources. After conducting a survey on what age a person would do the activities mentioned above, we arrived at an average mental age of forty.
4. Divide the mental age (40) by the chronological age (12). Forty divided by twelve is equal to 3.33 (40/12 = 3.33.)
5. Multiply the result of the previous division by one hundred to get the financial IQ. In this case it is 3.33 x 100 = 333.33.

Our financial IQ at the age of twelve was 333.33. In other words, we were over two hundred percent more productive than a conventional twelve-year-old and had a financial IQ equal to an average forty year old.

The reason why we show these three examples is to show you the great advantage that you give your children by providing them with financial education from an early age. Parents play an important role in the development of financial intelligence. Today we thank our parents for creating spaces and activities that helped educate us. We understand the great contribution of the long and intense Monopoly tournaments and the competitions of counting money in a limited time. Today we realize the importance of missing a day of school to go to work with our parents to learn daily business operations. If you are not a businessman, do not worry! There are still many ways to show your child how a company works, simply by applying some creativity. Always remember that happiness must prevail when elevating the financial IQ. The critical factor is turning learning into fun times you and your child can enjoy together.

When a person knows where they are going, the whole world opens the way. When a person does not know where they are going, the whole world gets in the way. Teaching your child to be confident of what they want is essential to prevent people from getting in their way and creating confusion in their decisions. The best way to show them a clear path and to prepare them for the future is by guiding them to start their financial education immediately! This way your children will develop their financial intelligence, which many children do not get a chance to develop due to lack of information.

Children and young people who have a high financial IQ tend to be more responsible, less vulnerable to manipulation, and have more options and opportunities for success in their professional and personal life as adults. We invite you to apply the financial IQ formula to your children and yourselves to monitor your productivity levels.

"IT IS POSSIBLE TO DEVELOP ENTREPRENEURSHIP SKILLS IN A FUN WAY WITH YOUR FAMILY"

CHAPTER 12
WHAT TIME IS IT?

In this last chapter, we were looking for ways to make parents understand what their children think and feel. We found that the best way was through a letter that consists of stories we collected from as many children as possible. So today, parents, we want to become the voice of your children. Perhaps some of the situations do not apply to your relationship with your children, but many children are currently going through all of the situations we depict. While you read, please think about your relationship with your child and ask yourself if it is time to change.

Hi Mom and Dad,

I'm writing this letter because I want to be happy. I am tired of looking for attention away from home. I may appear to have many friends, but we are not close. They are just people I know that I call my friends, so I feel less alone. Every day, I listen to my teachers, family and my supposed friends, when the only voice I really want to hear is yours. I want to know what you think of the real me, and not who I have become. You are the only one who can see beneath all the shields I create with my lies and false smiles. Only you can see the real me.

Alcohol is just one of the shields I use so that people do not see the real me. To tell you the truth, alcohol is not fun for me. I do not even understand how someone can really like it, but every time I get drunk I felt happy-for a little while. Recently, it stopped having the same effect on me. It did not cause the same feeling, so I decided to follow the advice of one of those friends that I never introduced to you, and I used drugs. Thanks to them, I could fool myself for a moment and feel happy again. I did it with friends, which made me feel important. The problem is that once they left, and the drugs wore off, the feeling of happiness vanished and depression invaded my heart. It was painful to realize that these had only a temporary effect and the heartbreaking truth was still there. Whenever I came home you were not there, or you were too tired to talk to me.

Laziness has become my new lifestyle. Every time I want to do something about my life, something productive, laziness wins.

I guess because I'm used to it and I am not strong enough to leave this comfort zone without responsibilities. My bed has become my confidant. It is where I leave all the tears I hide from everyone. If you ever want to really know how I feel, come to my room after an argument when I have shouted that I do not want to see you anymore and to leave me alone. Right in that moment, when I lock myself in my room so you cannot see me cry, is when I need you most. I take refuge in my room because I don't want you to think I'm weak, but actually loneliness and the idea of leaving this world to stop being a burden on the family invades me. When I look in the mirror and see my reflection, I do not recognize myself. At that moment, I would exchange every material thing you have ever given me for one of your hugs or at least a few words asking me if I am okay. Then I could finally say, "No I'm not, I need a hug!"

I'm tired of pretending to be strong. I'm tired of feeling like a burden to the family. I'm so tired of pretending to be happy. It hurts to see how other people can be truly happy and successful, and I can't. You know why? Because I'm afraid. I'm afraid of saying what I like, of sharing my ideas or dreams. I know I will not be able to achieve it. I thank you for taking your time to read these words. I needed you to know how I feel because every time I feel more pressure and I feel like not going to be able to continue resisting.

I have been writing this letter for days and practicing how to tell you everything I feel. When writing, my eyes flooded with tears because I realized that if I ever felt truly happy it was at your side. Remember all those times when I was little and I was really happy; when I did not have to fake a smile in front of your friends, and when I could not keep the tears from rolling down my cheeks from laughing uncontrollably? I remember you always said I was a happy little person, but today there is nothing left of that. I also remember the words you told me whenever I fell down, when you gave me your hand to help me get up and move on. I miss feeling that I am the greatest blessing in your life. Remember when you would tell me that every night, after you gave me a kiss on the forehead and told me to have sweet dreams? I miss feeling that you wanted to protect me, even from the nightmares that woke me up in the middle of the night.

I want to apologize for all the times I have been angry or upset you, when I said I did not want you in my life, or that you were the worst parents of all. Forgive me for all the things I've told you out of anger and frustration. Forgive me for leaving home in search of a fictitious happiness. Forgive me for those times you wanted to talk to me and I stared at my cellphone. Forgive me for thinking that the happiness I spoke of so much was in vices or in material things. The truth is that I used these excuses to defend myself from my own feelings. My arrogance and anger made me blind and didn't let me understand that the real reason you scolded me was because you were worried about what I was doing with my life. Sadness hardened my heart and I ended up thinking that all these vices were good and the bad guys in the story were Mom and Dad.

I never understood why my friends could be happy and I could not. I was filled with envy when they told me their happy stories of weekends with their parents. That is the reason I came home late. I did not want to be disappointed when I arrived and saw that you were not going to be available for me. I know I created stories and situations in my head that were maybe different from the reality. That is why I am writing to you today. With this letter, I am opening my heart to you in the most sincere way because it is destroyed, and it needs you. I need your help to restore confidence in myself because I want to be happy. I have never admitted it, but all those days of wasting my time, I really took a few moments to think about the dreams and goals I wanted to achieve. The problem is that I am afraid that my friends will make fun of me. What scares me more is to think you may think they are ridiculous. The truth is that I often tried to do better in school and begin to find my way again, but nothing I did worked. I understood everything in class, but when taking an exam, nerves got the best of me and everything I knew faded from my mind. For this reason, I need you by my side to give me strength whenever things do not turn out as planned. I need you to guide me, I need to hear and feel you love. I want to be someone in life. I want to become someone great and successful, someone for you to feel proud of.

I ask you not to leave me alone because you are the only company I need. I admire you as a person and as the leader you are at home. Maybe I never told you, but you have always been a role model for me. I only ask you not to leave me alone on this road. I want to change, for my family and myself. I finally understood that my actions and thoughts could not make you understand me; they were just destroying me. Please do not ignore my words. They are my last hope. Money, friends, and material things never filled my empty life. I only used them to *get away from the emptiness, but I realized that I was wrong. Only you can fill my heart. You are my world, my parents and I want you closer to me. Perhaps it sounds strange since the last time I said it, but it is the most important truth I have. With all my heart I want you to know that I LOVE YOU.*

Sincerely, Your child.

As difficult as some of the cases described in this letter may sound, each one is a reality for many young people today. In this letter, we present many of the things your children live every day and want to say but do not dare. Our ultimate goal is to show how the wellbeing, success, and happiness of your children depend on you. What is the point of living in constant arguments? After reading these situations, we decided it would be our mission to present parents a system, called "Entrepreneurship," to counteract all these negative situations. Entrepreneurship is a key tool for developing better communication with your children and keeping them focused on something productive they can enjoy.

The purpose of entrepreneurship is to build a comprehensive, well-rounded youth with a definite character and clear goals, who is ready to add value to their society. It is time to open your eyes and realize that your children are innate entrepreneurs who were born to achieve great things. It is time to take action, to encourage your children to develop all these skills and discover those that are still hidden. It is time to be at the same level as your child and become his friend and confident. It is time to put into action all the tools we have presented in this book. Forge an excellent relationship with your child and develop their full potential. It is time to start raising an entrepreneur child!

Today is the best day to start!

If you are convinced that children and young people have enormous potential, if you have made the decision to help them achieve their full potential, if you have decided to become his or her Parent and Coach, the following information will be very useful for you. Remember, time is the most precious treasure we have. Today is a good day to start raising your child into an entrepreneur. You can become one, too. Why not? We have prepared a list of business ideas that are easy to start and require little capital. This list was created with the intention of opening your minds and your children's as well, and providing you with a starting point. Today's young people are creators of the most amazing inventions. We want you to be open, not limited to the options presented in this list. Let your creativity and ingenuity dominate. Show your child several options and let them decide.

Business ideas for kids and young people

- Chocolates
- Bakery
- Event planning
- Organizing children's parties
- Pet care
- Recycling
- Bicycle rental

- Purchase and sale of textbooks
- Home makeovers
- Commercialization of technological products
- Renting video games
- Hikes and weekend trips
- Sale of handmade products, such as jewelry
- Custom clothing
- Photography
- Band
- Academy of art or music
- Florist or plant nursery
- Christmas ornaments
- Creating scrapbooks and albums
- Car washing
- Garden design and lawn care

Online business ideas for kids and young people

- Video editing
- Graphic design
- Digital marketing and administration of social networks
- Design of mobile applications and games
- Web design
- Tutorials
- Online auctions
- Blogs and Vlogs

Items for Consideration

- Money is not the most important thing in these cases. The experiences and lessons learned are. Do not demand economic goals or pressure your child based on financial issues.
- It is easy for a young person to get tired, want to give up, feel frustrated or change ideas often. It is in those moments where we need a word of encouragement and motivation. Teach the basics of discipline and perseverance, not only for business, but for life in general.
- Use the "failures" as learning moments and an opportunity to motivate your child. Tenacity and endurance are characteristics that an entrepreneur must develop. It is beneficial to learn these as we grow up and not face failure suddenly when we are adults.
- Take their ideas seriously and show interest in their proposals.
- Let them make and take responsibility for their own decisions; this will help them strengthen their self-esteem and encourage them to trust in their capacities.
- Help your child identify and overcome his or her fears. Motivate them to take calculated risks considering the pros and cons of every situation.
- Answer your child's questions with love. Place your knowledge and experience at their service without doing everything for them. Let them explore and find solutions to their problems.
- Challenge your child's capacity and implant the desire for constant improvement. Motivate them outside of their comfort zone and leave yours, as well. Look for alternative ways of doing things. Be creative and innovative.

- No matter what business your child decides to start, a key activity will always be present: sales! Practice with them. At first it may be difficult and awkward, but with practice and time, it will become easier and they will become better sellers.
- Be very patient. It is likely that many things will turn out unexpectedly; they will make mistakes. Be very careful in the way you address these situations. Do not make fun of their failed attempts or affect their feelings and self-esteem.

All of the above are tips for taking action immediately in the education of your children. Remember, according to Albert Einstein's definition, insanity is doing the same thing over and over again and expecting different results. So it is time to do different things in training your children to achieve different results in their lives. The way to success of your children will not be immediate. On the road there will be days when things will not go as planned, you will feel like what you are doing is not working, and you will feel anger. At other times you will feel joy and satisfaction, things will fall smoothly into place, and you will be grateful you took this chance. The truth is that all these feelings are necessary to know that you are on the right path. It is time to accept the challenge and leave behind all the things preventing you from taking action.

IT IS TIME TO START PARENTING AND COACHING AT THE SAME TIME!

How to Identify your Type of Brain

In this section you fill find the Triune Quotient Detector created by Waldemar de Gregori, which are used to identify your predominant, subdominant and third brain. There are three different types of test: one for adults, one for high school teenagers, and one for elementary school kids. The questions vary depending on the age of the person that is taking the test. This test will give you a quick insight into your brain's make up. Go back to Chapter 8 to review the information after taking this test.

Taking the test

To answer the test you have to rate each question with a number from 1 (which represents the minimum) to 5 (which represents the maximum), please do not use decimal numbers. You will have to put the number inside the geometric figure placed next to each question.

For example:

1) Do you evaluate or review your actions at the end of the day, week, or activity?

If you do an evaluation of your activities on a daily basis you should answer this question with a 5. If you do an evaluation on a bi-monthly basis you should answer this with a 3 or a 4. If you never do an evaluation of your activities you should answer this question with a 1.

You are supposed to answer this test with honesty and the truth about your life. If your answers are truthful and carefully considered, then your scores should be accurate.

Understanding the scores

After you've completed all 27 questions, add all the numbers inside the squares on the left column, then add all the numbers inside the triangles in the middle column, and finally all the numbers inside the circles on the right column. Your highest number indicates your dominant or strongest brain. The second highest number indicates your sub-dominant brain, and the lowest number indicates your weakest or third brain. The square represents the left part of the brain, the circle represents the right part of the brain and the triangle represents the central part of the brain. Now you've got the first glimpse of how your brain is structured.

Figure	Brain dominance
△	Central
○	Right
□	Left

TQ - TRIUNE QUOTIENT DETECTOR (Adults)

Write the answer to each question inside the corresponding geometric symbol (square, triangle or circle) figure. Rate each answer on a scale from 1 to 5 where 1 is the minimum and 5 is the maximum.

01	Do you stop for an evaluation or review at the end of the day, week, or activity?	□
02	Can you keep your house, your room, your work area in order?	△
03	Do you believe in something superior, spiritual?	○
04	Are you able to live joyously, optimistically, and enjoy everyday life?	○
05	In a dialogue or a debate, do you have good explanations, arguments to present and reflections to go deeper?	□
06	Do you have forebodings, premonitions, dreams that come true?	○
07	Do you approach romantic relationships with intensity, romanticism, and passion?	○
08	Do you know how to speak to an audience, using words fluently and correctly?	□
09	When talking, do you gesticulate, move your body, maintain direct eye contact with others?	○
10	Can you put yourself in somebody else's place and experience how that person might be feeling?	○
11	Can you ponder the pros and cons of a problem, discern them, and come up with the right decision?	□
12	When conveying a fact, can you put forth a good amount of detail?	□
13	When selling or buying, do you feel good about the results? Do you have any advantage? Do you make money?	△
14	Do you like innovation? Change in your routine, your environment? Do you have original, creative solutions?	○
15	Do you stop to think about the consequences before taking any action?	□
16	Before accepting the validity of any new information, do you take time to gather more data and to check the references?	□
17	Can you use needles, saws, hammers, screwdrivers, and other tools?	△
18	When facing a difficult task, do you have the ability to concentrate, to keep striving, to endure it?	△
19	As a boss, do you know how to divide tasks, establish a schedule, give precise commands and exercise control?	△
20	Do you take time to watch the sunset, a bird or a landscape?	○
21	Are you attracted by adventures, new tasks, or by actions that no one has ever done before?	△

22	Do you doubt the truthfulness of the news, politicians, religion, science?	□
23	Can you turn your dreams and ideals into realities that last and prosper?	△
24	Are you used to thinking about tomorrow, next year, the next ten years?	○
25	Is it easy for you to operate technology such as tape recorders, calculators, washers, computers, cars?	△
26	Are you faster than your colleagues in what you do? Do you always finish what you started?	△
27	When you communicate, do you use numbers, statistics, percentages, mathematics?	□

TOTALS (L)__(C)__(R)__

Scoring key:		
The lowest	The mean	The highest
9	28-35	45

TQ - TRIUNE QUOTIENT DETECTOR
(HIGH SCHOOL STUDENTS)

Write the answer to each question inside the corresponding geometric symbol (square, triangle or circle) figure. Rate each answer on a scale from 1 to 5 where 1 is the minimum and 5 is the maximum.

01	Do I check whether the details of a ticket or a bill are correct as soon as a get it?	□
02	Can I keep my room well organized and have everything in its place?	△
03	Do I believe that my body, my energy are part of a bigger whole, of any superior, invisible reality?	○
04	Am I joyful, optimistic, enthusiastic and easy to laugh?	○
05	When arguing do I have good explanations, good arguments, do I know how to respond?	□
06	When facing a difficulty, do I often come out with sudden insights, brilliant ideas?	○
07	Am I romantic and passionate when I fall in love?	○
08	When I communicate to people do I have enough arguments to persuade others about my point?	□
09	When talking, do you gesticulate, move your body, maintain direct eye contact with others?	○
10	How much can I put myself in somebody else's situation, imagine and feel his/her problems?	○
11	When facing a problem do I make a list of both favorable and unfavorable aspects to support my decision-making process?	□
12	When reporting something do I like to do it with plenty of details?	□
13	When selling, buying and negotiating do I have advantages?	△
14	Do I like to innovate and change the way things are done? Do I like to change my routine?	○
15	Before doing something, do I think of the consequences that action might bring? Do I have control over my emotions?	□
16	Before accepting the validity of news or gossips, do you go directly to the source to find out if it is true?	□
17	How good are you with manual habilities including handling needles, saws, hammers, screwdrivers, and other tools for domestic repairs?	△
18	When facing a difficult task, am I able to concentrate, keep trying and endure for a long time?	△
19	As a leader or when in charge of other people, do I know how to assign tasks, establish a schedule, give precise commands and exercise control?	△
20	How much is my attention captured by flowers, by a singing bird, a sunset or a beautiful landscape?	○
21	How much appeal do I have for adventures and actions that no one has ever done before?	△

22	How far do I go in my criticism regarding news reports, politicians, religion and science?	□
23	How often can I turn my dreams and ideals into successful realities?	△
24	How much time do I devote to thinking what will happen during the next 10,20 or 50	○
25	How good am I operating technology such computers, ipads, cameras, smartphones?	△
26	Do I always finish what I start within the established time?	△
27	When communicating, how much do I use numbers, percentages, math and statistics?	□

TOTALS (L)__(C)__(R)__

Scoring key:		
The lowest	The mean	The highest
9	28-35	45

TQ - TRIUNE QUOTIENT DETECTOR (ELEMENTARY SCHOOL STUDENTS

Write the answer to each question inside the corresponding geometric symbol (square, triangle or circle) figure. Rate each answer on a scale from 1 to 5 where 1 is the minimum and 5 is the maximum.

01	When watching or listening to something, do I try to concentrate and focus as much as possible?	□
02	How much do I engage in starting activities and having my friends involved in them?	△
03	Regarding my religion, do I have faith in something? Do I know how to pray?	○
04	How well can I tell jokes, solve puzzles, and find funny things to laugh at?	○
05	How much can I go along arguing with words and ideas without getting angry and fighting?	□
06	How good am I in guessing what is going to happen?	○
07	How much do I like other people and how much am I able to make others like me?	○
08	How good am I in asking questions?	□
09	When talking, do you gesticulate, move your body, maintain direct eye contact with others?	○
10	How well can I put myself in other people's situations and feel the way they feel?	○
11	How fast am I in noticing what is right and wrong with myself, at home and at school?	□
12	When asked "what happened today at school", am I able to answer with many and precise details?	□
13	When buying or interchanging things, do I have an advantage?	△
14	Do I like to change my routine and invent new ways of doing things?	○
15	How much do I think before taking an action or decision?	□
16	How much do I like studying and learning?	□
17	How good are my abilities for handcrafts?	△
18	How strong is my attention at school during classes?	△
19	How much do I care for my books, my toys and my stuff?	△
20	Do I like to dress well and have a good personal presentation?	○
21	In competitions, sports and games, how much do I strive to defeat my competitors?	△

22	When I think something is wrong, how much do I care to criticize it and to ask for the truth?	☐
23	When I have a goal, how hard am I willing to go to achieve it?	△
24	Do I take time to imagine how will be my life in the next 10 or 20 years?	◯
25	How good am I with video games, computers, iPads and technology?	△
26	How much do I like to be busy, doing things and/or helping at home?	△
27	Do I like math and numbers?	☐
	TOTALS	(L)__(C)__(R)__

Scoring key:		
The lowest	The mean	The highest
9	28-35	45

Mental Intensity Scoring Key

L	18 19 20 21 22 23 24 25 26 27	28 29 30 31 32 33 34	35 36 37 38 39	40 41 42 43 44 45
C	18 19 20 21 22 23 24 25 26 27	28 29 30 31 32 33 34	35 36 37 38 39	40 41 42 43 44 45
R	18 19 20 21 22 23 24 25 26 27	28 29 30 31 32 33 34	35 36 37 38 39	40 41 42 43 44 45
The lowest		The mean	Upper	The highest

References

Adolescentes Drogas Y Alcohol 3." Family Management. All Family Resources. Web. 16 Feb. 2016

Construcción Familiar- Escolar de los 3 cerebros. Waldemar de Gregori. 2002. Bogota, Colombia. (book)

"El Embarazo En La Adolescencia." OMS. Web. 16 Feb. 2014 EFE, and Reuters. "OMS: Cada 40 Segundos Una Persona Se Suicida En El Mundo."

Tendencias. La Tercera, 04 Sept. 2014. Web. 16 Feb. 2016 Guide to TRANCE- formation. Richard Bandler. 2008. Florida. (book)

"Interview: Sir Martin Sorrell: CEO, WPP." How Did They Do It. 2013. Web. 16 Feb. 2016.

Kiyosaki, Robert T. Rich Dad's Increase Your Financial IQ: Get Smarter with Your Money. New York: Business Plus, 2008. Print.

Kiyosaki, Robert T. Why "A" Students Work for "C" Students: And "B" Students Work for the Government. Scottsdale, AZ: Plata, 2013. Print

Licensed practitioner of neuro linguistic programming. Richard Bandler and John LaValle. 2011. (workbook of the seminar).

Licensed master practitioners of Neuro Linguistic Programming.

Richard Bandler and John La Valle. 2014. (Workbook of seminar).
Neuroeducación para el éxito. Waldemar de Gregori. 2014. (ebook).

Persuasion engineering. Richard Bandler and John La Valle. 2011. (workbook from a seminar).

The 7 Mindsets. Scott Schickler and Jeff Waller. 2012. (book)

The secrets of being happy. Richard Bandler and Garner Thomson. 2011. (book)

About the Authors

Karen, Daniela and Stephanie are 3 sisters who started their first business at the ages of 6,7 and 8 in Cartagena, Colombia and now reach the world with a powerful message of entrepreneurship. The Carvajalino sisters are young entrepreneurs, authors, trainers, motivational speakers, and investors. They started their first business with only $15 and today are owners of 4 successful companies. Chococar, a chocolate company, was their first adventure in the world of entrepreneurship. They sold their chocolates door to door in their neighborhood an later on, the success in sales took them to hire their first employee.

One year later, the sisters were invited to share their experience with an MBA class. Even though this represented a big challenge for them, the sisters decided to take it and that lead them to discover their passion for empowering others to follow their dreams and to believe in themselves. After speaking to hundreds and hundreds of people, the sisters founded Quality Line, a speaking and training company focused on developing an entrepreneurial mindset in their audiences and engaging them to generate sustainable, positive changes by applying Neuro Linguistic Programming, Triadic Brain techniques, dynamism and a big dose of energy.

By the ages of 13, 14 and 15 the sisters published their first book titled Parents and Coaches: The Best Strategic Alliance to Raise an Entrepreneur. This is the first book written from young entrepreneurs to parents in which the authors propose an innovative approach to children's financial education beginning at home and a way to develop their children's talents at an early age. Few years later, they created a family investment group that operates in different industries. In 2016, the three young ladies launched the revised version of their first book in which they added all the knowledge and an innovative methodology that supports their mission: to create a new generation of entrepreneurs that will create a true social and economic impact in our society. Today, the sisters continue to run their businesses and inspire thousands of people around the globe.

Connect With the Carvajalino Sisters

• Speaking Engagements
Quality Line is a groundbreaking speaking and training company that serves corporations, educators, students, parents and entrepreneurs. Are you interested in having Karen, Daniela and Stephanie at your event, convention or meeting? To book them visit www.qualitylinetraining.com or email info@qualitylinetraining.com

• Bulk Orders
Need to order books in bulk? Get awesome discounts for volume book orders. We can also arrange a book signing event or a Q&A session with the authors. For more information email info@parentsandcoaches.com

• Entrepreneurship Program for Youth
Biz Nation is an entrepreneurship program that introduces and guide its students to the exciting world of creating and owning a business. This program provides organizations with all the material, guidance and support needed to establish an entrepreneurial life-changing experience for the youth. For a customized quote email info@parentsandcoaches.com

• Interviews
For media and press related inquiries please contact info@parentsandcoaches.com

If you have any questions or comments please direct them to info@parentsandcoaches.com or visit www.parentsandcoaches.com.

Facebook: Hermanas Cavajalino
Instagram: hermanascavajalino
Twitter: @LasCarvajalino